Equitation Safety

Equitation Safety

Everything about your safety in connection with horses

Jan Ladewig

Black Tent Publications

www.blacktent.co.uk

First published in 2015
by
Black Tent Publications
145 Durham Road
Stockton-on-Tees
TS19 0DS

www.blacktent.co.uk

Editing and design by Lesley Skipper

Printed & bound by
Lightning Source UK Ltd.
Chapter House
Pitfield
Kiln Farm
Milton Keynes
MK11 3LW

ISBN: 978-1-907212-16-1

A catalogue record for this book is available from the British Library

The book is dedicated to my daughter, Freja: May you always stay healthy and happy around horses.

Contents

Rock carving from Tanum, Sweden, from the Bronze Age (1700–500 BC)

Foreword

BY ANDREW MCLEAN

EVER since the horse was first domesticated sometime around the end of the 2nd millennium BC., it has served various functions for humankind. Initially pulling battle wagons for war and as beasts of burden for transport and agriculture, the modern horse's role has only recently changed in the developed world to largely one of leisure and sporting pursuits. With this change in role, the safety aspects have become even more paramount, particularly with the proliferation of pony club and other equine activities for children. Yet despite these changes, knowledge of horse training and management has largely filtered down to us from tradition, including many of the myths and misconceptions that can render the horse more dangerous, which poses a large threat to both human and horse welfare.

The safety statistics of horse-human interactions are staggering: the horse is easily the most dangerous animal in the Western world. While the human death rate is as high as one death per million head of population, the serious injury rate is 20 times greater than motorcycling: one serious injury for every 350 hours of contact. Moreover, research shows that children suffer more life-threatening head and neck injuries than adults. We have a moral obligation to do a better job of understanding the true nature of horses, including their training and management. More precisely, information is needed at the 'grass-roots' level so that current scientifically proven knowledge can make the horse world a safer place to be for both people and horses.

Equitation Safety fills that void. It is unique in its scope, scientific accuracy and simplicity. It should be compulsory reading for all horse owners, particularly those new to the horse world and those who have children who ride or intend to ride horses and ponies. The breadth of vision for this book is vast and would seem rather daunting were it not for the fact that it is so easy to read. Every imaginable topic is thoroughly covered and important yet controversial topics are dealt with according to the current scientific literature. Issues of dominance and respect are rightfully questioned and replaced with solutions for achieving behaviour change and training goals. Notions of leadership are also debunked convincingly. Fundamental instinctive behaviours are explained with regard to their relevance to horse handling and management. Learning processes ranging from habituation to reinforcement and learning by association are also explained in a way that people uninitiated in such topics will readily grasp.

From the practical point of view, *Equitation Safety* is rich in very sound advice. Not only does it tell you how to load a horse into a trainer, but it also tells you how to load and unload difficult or inexperienced horses and then even how to hitch up the vehicle! The book also outlines important yet often overlooked issues, such as what to look for when buying a horse, particularly with respect to suitability and safety. It explains how to clean out hooves, advice on riding unknown horses and sufficiently in-depth information on how to actually train the horse right from the start in foundation training.

Equitation Safety

Equitation Safety is arguably the most thorough safety examination of horse-human interactions available. Throughout the book, the risks of every interaction are described and then responded to with solutions on minimising the risks. One of the a great attributes of this book is that the information is presented in a systematic way so that when riders or handlers have problems or have achieved certain levels in training they can take the book and read the relevant section and then go back and train or retrain the horse.

In an age where animals are humanised more than ever and pseudo-science gives the false impression that animals such as horses are willing-to-please beings, this book is refreshingly honest and pragmatic. The importance of control is strongly woven in the text throughout, yet without diminishing or disaffecting the bond between human and horse that is the very substance of the incredible relationships between our two species.

This text should be compulsory for equine science, equine therapy as well as equestrian and pony club federations and coaching courses. If horse people followed the advice in this book, there would most certainly be far fewer injuries to both horses and people and there would be much happier horses and people too. As a horseman and behavioural scientist myself, I am in the fortunate position to be able to say that there is nothing in this book that I disagree with and I unequivocally support the entirety of the book.

Professor Ladewig is unique in his qualifications and background to write such a text. Not only is he a leading academic scholar with vast range of peer-reviewed publications to his credit, but he is also a practical horseman, having ridden and trained horses from the early stages to more advanced training levels.

Equitation Safety is an important book. I strongly feel that it will significantly add to the safeguarding of both human and equine welfare throughout the world.

Andrew McLean holds a PhD in equine cognition and learning, has been an accredited horse riding coach for over 30 years and has written 5 books (including an International Best Seller) and authored 35 peer-reviewed journal articles. He developed and manages the Australian Equine Behaviour Centre, the most internationally recognised horse training and behaviour modification centre in Australia. He is also a member of the International Society for Equitation Science.

Preface

EVER since I met Gwenda over 55 years ago I have been interested in how to work with horses in such a way that neither I nor the horse got hurt. Gwenda was a New Forest pony that came to the riding school where I was riding when I was a child. I do not know what Gwenda had been through earlier in her life but she was extremely scared of people. If she could not escape them she would attack them, biting or kicking to avoid them. It took me half a year's daily work to change her opinion of humans in general and of me in particular. The experience of how to get from A to B without any major mishaps brought me into the fascinating world of how to train horses in a way that not only is safe for horse and person, but also in a way that creates trust in the horse.

Teaching a horse not to be scared of people or some of the many strange things people do is a unique opportunity to get an idea of how the mind of the horse works. You cannot help noticing what catches their attention. You soon find out how far you can go when exposing them to something scary so that they still remain relatively calm. And you learn very early on that rewarding them when they do something right is the best (and only) way to teach them instead of punishing them when they do something wrong.

Since those early days I have worked with numerous horses both as a veterinarian and as a rider. Many of those horses have shown me some of the risky situations that are so hard to avoid. And often I have done things that were not too smart. Together, however, we managed to get through the various activities relatively unscarred and to learn from the experience.

Learning from experience is one way to acquire information about equitation safety. Another way is to learn from other people's experience. Considering the risk involved, the latter way is definitely the best. And that has been my motive for writing this book. If sharing my experience could mean that just one rider (but hopefully a few more than that) would benefit from it and NOT have an accident, it will certainly have been worthwhile.

ACKNOWLEDGEMENTS

IT was not just horses that helped me write the book. My colleagues Dr. Janne Winther Christensen and Professor Frank Ödberg and my friend (who helped me with Gwenda) Ellen Shepherd McKee proofread earlier versions of the manuscript. Karsten Østergaard assisted in getting an electronic version (in Danish) on the market. Luise Thomsen, Epona.tv, took some of the pictures, and lastly Lesley Skipper, editor at Black Tent Publications corrected some of the many mistakes I had made in earlier versions of the manuscript. Thanks to all for your help.

Thanks also to the riders in some of the pictures.

Equitation Safety

Line Peerstrup Ahrendt, Jody Hartstone, Freja Munck Ladewig, and Mia Rosenlyst.

Part 1 General information about horses and equitation

Chapter 1

Equitation safety

ACCORDING to the statistics horse riding is one of the most dangerous of sports. In the USA, more than 100,000 riders need medical care yearly (in the UK, this figure is around 4,000). Undoubtedly, a much larger number of riders experience accidents that do not require medical care but often with the result that they end up being afraid of horses. Most horses are generally very gentle animals but they are flight animals whose safest defence against danger is to flee as fast as possible. This reaction, which is almost a reflex, is very sensible under natural conditions. Under husbandry conditions, however, it constitutes a risk when handling and riding horses. One of the main reasons why so many accidents happen is that riders are unaware of the many dangers that exist when working with horses.

> **The purpose of this riding safety book is to teach you to work around horses in a way that neither you nor your horse are hurt**

Working around a horse does not only mean to ride the horse. The largest part of the work with horses consists of taking care of them when we are not riding them. One third of all accidents do not happen when we ride horses. They happen when we take care of them.

Riding safety is not only a question of training and handling horses in the right way. Riding safely is also a question of how the horse is stabled. Luckily, more and more horses spend time together with other horses, either because they are kept in a loose housing system or because they are turned out daily in pasture together with other horses. The social contact with other horses is important not only because it is an innate need of horses, but also because it makes them more harmonious and, consequently, easier for the rider to handle. But to be able to go into a group of horses and catch the one you want to ride without getting hurt demands a much greater knowledge of horses than if your horse is standing alone in its own stable.

STRUCTURE OF THE BOOK

To ride and to handle horses in a safe way you need

◊   to be a good rider

◊   to know how horses react

◊   to know some of the dangerous situations that can happen when working with horses.

How you get to be a good rider (if you are not already one) is described in the section **Riding safety – the basic principles of the book** (page 19).

Knowledge of how horses react is described in the sections **The behaviour of the horse in relation to safety** (page 30) and **Training the Horse to be safe** (page 52).

What may constitute dangerous situations is described in seven sections:

Horses in pasture
Horses in the stable
Riding
Riding in the riding arena
Riding cross country
Riding problem horses
Trailer and lorry transportation of horses

Each section describes different conditions or situations that are risky and that can hurt you.

In each situation is described

1.   Why the situation may be risky

2.   What you can do to minimize the risk

3.   What you should do or not do if a dangerous situation happens

Important things are mentioned in a box like this.

Specially important things, for instance things that can be dangerous and things you absolutely should know are placed next to a warning sign.

In addition, some safety related advices (**First aid** (page 82), **In case of fire** (page 84), **Buying a horse from a safety-related point of view** (page 87), **To parents of a child interested in horses** (page 88)) are given in Chapters 5 and 6.

Liability: The author and publishers can accept no liability for injuries or accidents sustained as a result of the exercises and the training described in this book. In case of questions, contact the author.

RIDING SAFETY – THE BASIC PRINCIPLES OF THE BOOK

The book is based on the following two principles:

1.   That the rider has full control over his or her horse in all situations

2.   That the horse is able to fulfil its natural needs when left by itself

1. That the rider has full control over his or her horse in all situations means that the horse must learn to obey the commands of the rider in all situations, whether the rider sits on the horse, leads it, or stands next to it grooming it. The horse must learn to obey in the stable, when it is picked up from the pasture, when it is ridden in the indoor arena or outdoors, alone or together with other horses and riders.

> **Only if the rider has full control over the horse is it safe to ride and to handle.**

How you teach your horse to obey your commands, is described in the section **Training of horses,** page 52.

2. That the horse is able to fulfil its natural needs when left by itself, either in the stable or out in pasture means that it is fed the right feed, both concentrates and roughage, that it has water, and that it has the opportunity to rest and to be together with other horses.

> **Only if the horse can fulfil its physiological and behavioural needs can we with good conscience demand that it obeys us when it is together with us.**

How a horse fulfils its different behavioural needs is described in the sections **The behaviour of the horse in relation to safety** (page 30) and **Pasture** (page 49).

You should never be alone when you work with a horse. You should always have somebody near who could help you if you should need it.

Safe riding

To work with and to ride on a horse in a safe way, the most important fact is that you become a good rider.

◊ You become a good rider by riding frequently, preferably more than once a week, by receiving riding instruction, and by becoming an all-round rider and learning to ride dressage, jumping and cross country.

◊ If possible, you will profit from riding different horses. Getting used to the ways different horses move and react will make you a more experienced rider.

◊ You need to be in good physical shape so that you can keep your balance on the horse and so that you can interact with the horse in the right way. To ride a horse does not mean to be passively transported around. To ride safely on a horse you must be able to interact with it in a way that makes it obey without protesting.

To become a good rider you must

◊ get riding instruction

◊ get to know your horse

◊ learn to control your horse

◊ have the appropriate riding equipment

An important requirement for riding in a safe way is to learn to ride correctly. To stay in the saddle under all conditions, you need to learn to sit relaxed in the saddle, yet be prepared to press your knees together should something happen.

You must develop your ability to keep your balance on the horse, especially when it suddenly turns around or jumps sideways. The only way to develop that ability is by riding.

The better you are at staying in the saddle when your horse jumps over obstacles, the greater is your chance of staying in the saddle when your horse spooks and jumps away from something scary. And if a gallop cross country is something you do voluntarily once in a while, a gallop because your horse got scared of something is less likely to frighten you.

> **The rule about getting riding instruction accounts for all riding disciplines**

The rule is also true if you

◊ are a 'Sunday rider'

◊ ride Icelandic horses

◊ ride classical dressage

◊ are a Western rider

If, for instance, you are the kind of rider who just enjoys a ride in the woods, it is just as important that you have the necessary control over your horse and that you are able to stay in the saddle if it should get scared.

Riding ability

◊   You must not allow others to force you to ride faster, jump higher or to ride through a more difficult area than you feel you and your horse can manage.

◊   Another matter is that you should work on achieving more and more. But it must be done in a way that you feel reasonably comfortable with.

◊   Do not take any chances.

◊   If you get into a situation that you do not feel comfortable with, you need to proceed in a different way. If, for instance, your horse does not want to pass a certain place because it is scared, and you are afraid that it will rear or run away, it is better to get off your horse and lead it by, or to take a different route. Do not feel that you absolutely must 'take up the fight' with the horse. Some horses become calm if the rider gets off and lead it pass the scary place. Other horses may be more difficult to handle when you are on the ground.

When several riders are riding cross country, the least experienced rider sets the tempo. The more experienced riders should not ride in such a way (ride faster, jump obstacles, or the like) that the less experienced rider cannot manage. The more experienced riders must consider the ability of the less experienced rider so that everybody has a positive experience.

> **Show consideration for less experienced riders when you ride out together**

◊   Riding is sport that should be nice to participate in.

◊   Riding should be a positive activity for both horse and rider.

◊   If this is not the case, there is something seriously wrong.

Knowledge of horses

You must get to know your horse. Besides knowing about horse behaviour in general, you must also know about the behaviour of your own horse. The best way to obtain that knowledge is to go through the training described in this book. When you expose your horse to the situations mentioned here, you do not only habituate it to certain situations. You also learn how your horse reacts, whether it rears or turns around and runs off, or whether it remains standing still and considers the situation. And this knowledge will make you a better rider, especially a better rider of *your* horse.

To know how your horse reacts in different situations is worth a lot because you are better prepared for what can happen.

Control over your horse

Safe riding means that you have full control over your horse. As long as your horse is together with you, it must obey you. You are the one who makes the decisions. Only if you have full control over your horse is it safe to ride and to handle. But to obey a person is something that the horse must learn. It is not an innate characteristic.

How you make your horse obey is described in the section **Training the horse to be safe** (page 52).

As long as your horse is together with you, whether you sit on its back or you stand or walk beside it, IT IS YOU WHO MAKES THE DECISIONS

But you also need to realize that the fact that *you* are the one who decides what the horse should do, is not bad for the horse. On the contrary, it makes it feel safe. The clearer the horse knows what is allowed and what not, the safer it feels and the calmer it will be.

> **To demand that your horse obeys your commands in the right way does not only mean that the horse is safer to work with. It also makes it feel safer.**

Equitation Safety

To make the rules and to demand that the horse always follows them is similar to obedience training of your horse. Through the obedience training the horse learns habits that make the daily work easier and, most importantly, safer.

To obedience train your horse means to teach it good habits. Good habits you teach it during the training so that your horse always does what it has learned. But at the same time that your horse learns good habits, you yourself learn good habits, so that the daily work is nothing but a continuation of what you have practiced during the training.

But in order for your horse to consider your control over it as something positive, it must be allowed to be a horse when you are not around and it is left by itself. To be a horse means that it is able to relax together with other horses, for instance by spending as much time as possible in a pasture together with other horses (see the section **Pasture**, page 49).

> **To spend time on a pasture every day has a direct positive effect on how safe your horse is to handle and to ride.**

Equipment

You need to have your equipment in order:

◊ You must always ride with a riding helmet.

◊ You must wear solid footwear.

◊ It is a good idea to wear a safety vest.

◊ It is a good idea to wear gloves.

◊ It is a good idea to ride with safety stirrups.

◊ When you ride outdoors, you need to have your mobile phone on you plus connection with somebody who can come and help you, if it should be necessary.

> **Remember: Safety equipment may reduce the risk of you being seriously injured. Safety equipment cannot prevent you from having a riding accident.**

Riding helmet

◊ Your riding helmet should have a strong strap around your chin so that the helmet stays on your head if you should fall off.

◊ Your riding helmet should be of the right size, neither too large nor too small, and it should be sufficiently padded.

Footwear

◊ You must always have solid heeled shoes or boots on when you are around horses. Sandals and sneakers are not good enough. Even if a small pony steps on your toes, you can easily break a toe.

◊ Boots with toe protection are the best as long as the toe protection is sturdy enough to bear the weight of a horse.

◊ Remember that the stirrups must fit the size of your boots. If the stirrup is too big, your foot can slip through. If it is too small, your foot can get stuck in the stirrup.

Safety vest

◊   A safety vest is good to wear, even when you are not riding. If you fall off the horse a safety vest protects your back. Spinal lesions are a frequent outcome of riding accidents.

◊   But the safety vest also protects you, if for instance you receive a kick on your chest or if a horse pushes you against a wall.

Gloves

◊   Gloves protect your hands, especially when you lead your horse with a rope.

◊   Wearing gloves means that you have a better grip on the rope so that you are less likely to wrap the rope around your hand.

◊   Gloves also give you a better grip on the reins when you are riding.

◊   Gloves also protect your hands in other situations, such as when you clean hooves.

You must <u>**NEVER**</u> **wrap rope, reins, or lunge line around your hand, arm or any other part of your body. You must only be connected with your horse in such a way that you can instantly come free of the horse.**

Things you ABSOLUTELY must not do:

Rope around wrist or arm
Lunge line around body
Reins around neck

Safety stirrups

Using stirrups with a rubber band on one side prevents you from getting your foot stuck in the stirrup in case you should fall off the horse. But make sure that the rubber band is not old and cracked so that you lose it during your ride.

Another safety device for stirrups is toe-stoppers that are fastened to the stirrups and that prevent your foot from sliding too far into the stirrup.

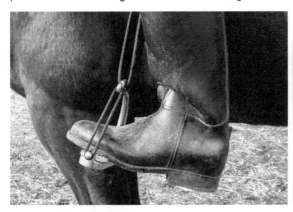 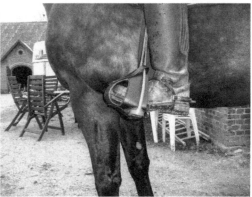

Stirrup with rubber band. Remember that the rubber band must sit on the outside. Remember to bring a spare rubber band when riding out cross country.

Mobile phone

◊ The best safety equipment to have along (except for the riding helmet), both when riding indoors and outdoors, is a mobile phone. But the phone is only helpful if there is somebody you can call and who can help you if it should become necessary. If you are riding out, you must be able to explain where you are. That is why it is a good idea to let somebody know where you are going before riding out.

◊ On the other hand, you should only use the phone in emergency. Talking with your friends takes away your concentration from the ride so that you are less aware of what is going on in your surroundings. And that is not good when sitting on a horse.

◊ And remember: keep the phone in your pocket and not in a saddlebag. You will not be able to call for help if your horse has run off with your telephone!

Maintenance of saddle and bridle

◊   Riding equipment must be maintained to prevent the leather from drying out. Dry leather such as stirrup straps or reins can crack. If that happens during a canter or during a jump, you can get seriously hurt.

◊   If the damage has already happened, you need to change the leather part before riding out.

Maintenance of the safety lock that carries the stirrup strap

◊   The safety lock on the saddle bar is normally turned up as in the picture. It works in the way that, if the rider falls off and his foot gets stuck in the stirrup, it opens up from the weight of the rider so that the stirrup strap slides off the saddle.

◊   But the safety lock only works if it is maintained and oiled regularly and if the rider is heavy enough.

◊   When children are sitting in the saddle, it is safer to unlock it.

◊   When it is unlocked the risk of the stirrup strap sliding off is greater if the rider's leg is pulled backwards as often happens during jumping.

◊   To avoid that, it is better to lock it during jumping.

Jewellery

One thing that should not be part of your equipment is jewellery, such as finger rings, bracelets, necklaces, and earrings. They can all easily get caught in buckles and other parts of the riding gear, so that you get seriously hurt.

Chapter 2

The behaviour of the horse in relation to safety

AN important prerequisite for handling your horse in a safe way is to know

◊ how horses generally react in different situations

◊ how *your* horse reacts in different situations

The purpose of this chapter is to describe those behaviour patterns of horses that are relevant to the safety of riding on, and working with, horses.

To learn about how your horse reacts in different situations you can do when you go through some of the exercises described under **Training the horse to be safe** (page 52).

You need to realize that domestic horses, that is those horses and ponies that we ride, show almost the same behaviour as their wild ancestors. Even though people have kept horses for thousands of generations and in that time have bred horses for certain characteristics, the behaviour of domestic horses is almost completely similar to the behaviour of wild horses.

 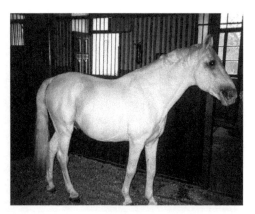

Above left: Przewalski horse: the closest relative of the domestic horse. Above right: Lipizzan horse.

If domestic horses are released into the wild, they quickly form social groups and are able to survive in the same way that wild horses do. The behaviour patterns that enable them to survive in nature (for instance to protect themselves against predators, to find food and water, and to reproduce) have not changed much despite the fact that most domestic horses look very different from wild horses.

Because the behaviour of domestic horses is the same as that of wild horses, they have the same behavioural needs. They need to be with other horses. They need to be out in the open. And they need to graze or eat many hours a day.

The more a horse gets its behavioural needs fulfilled, the more harmonious it is and the safer it is to be around.

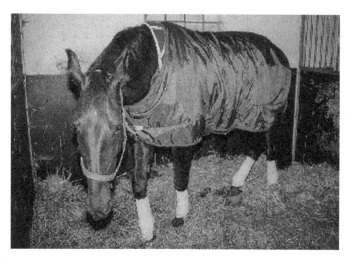

To stand in a stable alone for 23 hours out of the 24 hours is not natural for a horse.

Horses' flight behaviour

Horses are pronounced flight animals. Under natural conditions they live in open grassland where they are exposed to attacks from predators. In contrast to other prey animals (such as cattle that have horns) their only effective defence against natural enemies is to detect them as early as possible and to run away the very second there is danger. Only if it is not possible to flee will a horse defend itself by kicking or biting.

A horse that is surprised by some threat reacts in a fraction of a second by jumping to the side, turning around and, if it is sufficiently frightened, by running away as fast as possible. This reaction that is almost a reflex is very appropriate under natural conditions because the horse has a much better chance of avoiding a predator. Its chance of survival is greater. It is a characteristic that has been passed on for thousands of generations and it has not changed during the relatively short time that horses have served mankind.

The fast reactions of horses and their ability to run fast over longer distances are exactly those characteristics that have made them so valuable for us people. It was those characteristics that throughout history enabled us to travel far and to transport goods over continents.

Even though we have other means of travelling and transporting goods today, we still require horses to react fast, to run at great speed, and to jump high. And that is probably the main reason why the natural flight behaviour is not different in riding horses and in wild horses. Even though people have protected horses against wolves and other predators for thousands of years, they still have their innate propensity to jump away from something dangerous.

Przewalski horses watching a predator

The best defence of horses against natural enemies is

◊   to detect the danger as early as possible

◊   to flee at the least suspicion that danger is near

Senses

The senses of horses are well developed to detect danger. This is particularly true of

◊   the sense of vision

◊   the sense of hearing

◊   the sense of smell

Horses' vision

It is believed (but not agreed upon by everybody) that the eye of a horse is not round like in people, but oval. This should mean that a horse can see far away and close up simultaneously, in contrast with our eye that has to adapt to see things either far away or close up. Only a small area right in front of a horse's nose is blind.

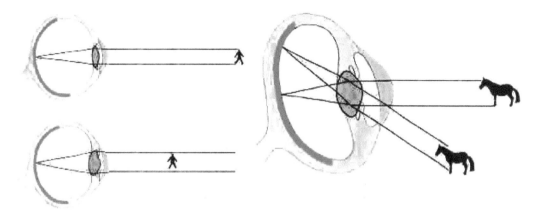

The eyes of a horse are located on the side of its head. That means that it can see almost all the way around itself. Only its own body prevents it from seeing things behind it, but it only has to turn the head slightly in order to also see this area.

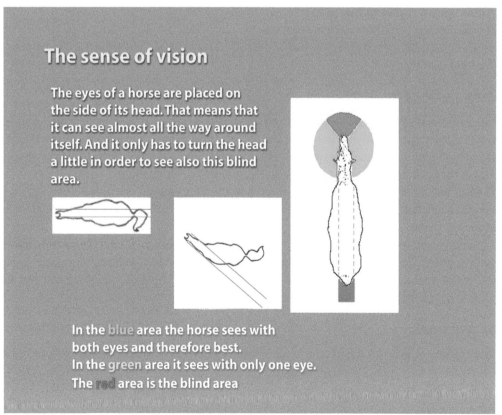

The sense of vision

The eyes of a horse are placed on the side of its head. That means that it can see almost all the way around itself. And it only has to turn the head a little in order to see also this blind area.

In the blue area the horse sees with both eyes and therefore best.
In the green area it sees with only one eye.
The red area is the blind area

Both the shape of the eye and its position on the head means that the horse can keep an eye on a large area, both nearby and far away. On the other hand, the picture it sees is not nearly as detailed as the picture we see. Objects that do not move are not easily detected by horses. Not until they move will the horse see them. When the wind is blowing, many things move. Leaves and branches swing around and make rustling sounds which can make a horse nervous.

If you are riding through the woods and you are approaching some deer standing grazing, the deer will see you first because you are moving. If you pay attention to things around you, you will also soon see the deer. But your horse will not see them until they start running away. If your horse is prone to be scared of wildlife fleeing through the woods, you can prepare yourself for the reaction of your horse *before* it reacts, simply because you see the 'danger' first.

Horses' hearing

Horses can direct their ears towards a sound. This means that they are good at localizing a sound. It is believed that the direction of the ears indicate where the focus of their vision is. When you ride your horse you may notice that it goes with one ear pointing forward and one pointing backward. It is believed that the horse 'keeps an eye on' both the signals from the rider and the area in front of it.

To hear sound means to detect the vibrations of the sound waves in the air. But horses are also able to detect vibrations in the ground. If prey animals nearby (for instance oxen) flee, their flight can be felt far away. To detect that kind of vibration means that their flight works as an alarm for other prey animals, a signal that there is danger nearby.

The floor of the horse trailer driving down the road vibrates. The same thing happens on a bridge when the horse walks over it. This is possibly the reason why horses do not like to stand and to walk on that kind of floors.

Horses' sense of smell

Horses' sense of smell is just as well developed as dogs' sense of smell. Horses can smell if some manure comes from a horse that they know or from an unfamiliar horse, if the manure is from a stallion or from a mare. Stallions can smell if a mare is in heat (in oestrus). Stallions can probably also judge how strong another stallion is by smelling the level of testosterone in his manure.

The fact that horses' senses in some areas are better developed than our senses and in other areas function in a different way than our senses means that horses experience their surroundings differently from the way we do.

To punish a horse for 'carrying on when there is no reason' is not just. It could be that the horse had sensed a possible danger that we had not detected. In this case it would be better to give the horse the benefit of the doubt, to calm it down like we would do if it was scared of something real, but also to demand that it continues to go forward, to stand still, or whatever it was doing earlier.

Fear reactions

A horse that gets scared of something may show several different fear reactions that you need to recognize as a rider.

1. The first reaction is that the horse lifts its head so that it is better able to orient itself.
2. At the same time it directs both eyes and ears towards the thing that scares it.
3. It widens its nostrils,
4. and lifts its tail. The tail lifting is a sign of tension in its body.
5. The horse starts to walk in a 'stiff' way.
6. If the horse is very frightened it may snort, that is blowing out air forcefully.

Depending upon how frightened the horse is, it may show only some of the symptoms. When it becomes aware of a potential danger (a sound or something moving), it directs its attention towards the place (1 and 2). If its suspicion continues, it becomes tense (1, 2, 3, and 4). Thereafter it starts to move around and to snort (5 and 6).

The more intense signs of fear, particularly the snorting, can act as a warning signal to other horses. If a horse in a group snorts, the whole group may immediately be frightened.

Two things are important to know about horses' fear reactions:

1. Each and every horse can be frightened
2. The flight reaction of a horse is activated like a reflex

Even a well-trained horse that has been habituated to cars, dogs, running children, plastic, and numerous other things and situations, can still be frightened by something. The horse may react automatically by fleeing. It is almost impossible to train a horse never to show flight behaviour.

Some riders claim that they do not need to use a riding helmet because their horse is so well trained that it is never frightened and therefore never shows flight reactions. This is nonsense!

Any horse can be frightened and, if that happens, the most well-trained horse will show a flight reaction.

Horses under a rider show flight behaviour by

◊ jumping to the side

◊ turning around and bolting

◊ possibly rearing

When a horse reacts by showing flight behaviour, there is only one way to stay in the saddle:

◊ to press the knees together

◊ to sit deep in the saddle (that is, upright or leaning slightly backwards, not leaning forwards)

◊ and to follow the movement of the horse as well as possible.

It takes a lot of lessons, a lot of cross country riding and, preferably, jumping exercises, in order to keep one's balance when the horse reacts in this way.

Because a horse can be scared any time and in all situations it is important always to sit on it as if it were going to jump forward or to the side. In other words, never sit too relaxed on your horse.

It is important to realize that horses react according to their nature when they jump to the side or bolt. But it is equally important to know that it is possible to change their tendency to react.

We cannot change the innate need to flee when frightened, but to a large extent we can change the horse's perception of what is dangerous and what is not. In other words, through training we can teach the horse not to run away when a truck comes driving, when a barking dog comes running, or when similar situations happen.

> **We cannot change a horse's need to flee when it is frightened, but we can change its perception of what is dangerous and what is not.**

The way to do so is to habituate the horse to as many things and situations that can frighten a horse as possible. The process is described in the section **Training the horse to be safe** (page 52).

Fear reactions and accidents

There are three ways to avoid a serious accident caused by the fear reactions of a horse:

1. You must try to avoid frightening the horse.
2. You must always be prepared for the risk that your horse is frightened and bolts.
3. You must habituate your horse to as many scary things and situations as possible.

If you fulfil these three needs you will reduce the risk of having an accident as much as possible.

1. Avoid frightening the horse:

◊   Avoid sudden movements and strange sounds.

◊   When you approach a horse, warn it that you are coming by talking to it.

◊   Do not run near horses. Teach children to be calm around horses.

◊   Be careful with unusual things around horses (for instance plastic bags, umbrellas, the flash from a camera).

2. Be prepared if your horse is frightened:

◊   When you ride it you must sit on it in such a way that you have as much contact with it as possible, particularly with your knees.

◊   If you ride with loose reins, do it in such a way that you can grab them and stop the horse in an instant (see **Riding with loose reins,** page 129).

◊   When you lead your horse you must hold the lead rope or the reins in such a way that you can let go of it instantly. You must never wrap it around your hand or arm.

◊   If you stand near a loose horse you should stand sufficiently far enough away so that it does not jump into you if it bolts.

◊   When you stand close to a horse, you should have a halter or a bridle on it.

3.   Habituate your horse to things and situations that frighten horses

◊   As you can read in the section **Training** you should habituate your horse to as many different things as possible, such as cars, motor cycles, plastic, something dragging behind the horse, and numerous other things.

◊   The more strange things to which the horse is exposed, the less inclined it will be to become frightened by novel things.

◊   A horse that has been habituated to many different things is less inclined to become frightened. That is the reason why an older horse is usually calmer than a younger horse. It has more experience with meeting unknown things.

Do not punish a scared horse

If a horse is really scared or nervous of some object or some place and the rider interprets the fear reaction of the horse as disobedience and punishes it, the horse actually has its fear confirmed. There really was a good reason to be frightened!

> **To punish a horse for being frightened does not make it less fearful. On the contrary.**

Instead, let the horse stop and give it time to investigate the object or the place. After a short time you can start demanding that it calmly continues what you were doing.

SOCIAL BEHAVIOUR OF HORSES

Horses are herd animals. The chance of survival in nature is greater when horses live in a herd.

◊   The risk of being killed by a predator is smaller when other horses are present

◊   The chance that a predator nearby is discovered is greater, the more horses are together in a herd

The need for domestic horses to be together with other horses is as great as in wild horses. The need for social contact (also called the herd instinct) has not changed despite the fact that horses live under the protection of people.

The fact that horses feel safer in the company of other horses we can use to our advantage when we want to habituate the horse to something new and unfamiliar. See how in the section **Habituation**, page 59.

Despite the fact that horses feel safest in a group, the coexistence with other horses also means increased competition (for instance over feed) that can result in a fight. Undoubtedly, competitive situations are much more frequent in domestic horses living under more restriction than wild or feral horses. Because of the higher frequency of threats and fights, it is a common belief that horses form a social hierarchy or a social rank order in order to reduce or avoid aggression. It is further commonly believed that the animal on top of the hierarchy (the alpha animal) usually is one of the older and more experienced horses of the herd.

Horses may threaten or fight with each other but this happens on a one to one basis. They may learn that a specific horse is stronger (or weaker) when it comes to who gets the hay first. If the group in which they live is relatively small they may learn this information about all the members in the group. These 'bilateral' relationships, however, do not mean that the horses have an overall plan or a structure of them. Although horses have been shown to possess much greater cognitive abilities than has generally been supposed, it is unlikely that they think of their relationships in terms of such a plan. That seems to be something that only humans do. In addition, being stronger in one situation (for instance when competing over food) does not necessarily mean that the horse is also stronger in another situation (for instance getting home from the pasture first).

Similarly, the concept of leadership is also doubtful. In wild or feral horses, any member of the group can take the initiative to go somewhere. If for instance, a young horse in a group starts wandering off to the watering place, some of the other horses in the group may start walking after the young horse and after a while the whole group may follow. It may also happen that nobody starts to follow the young horse. If that is the case it will turn around and go back to the group. Obviously, in this and similar situations there is no indication of any form of leadership.

When horses compete they mostly do so by threatening each other. The threat can consist of:

1. Sending a threatening stare.
2. Swishing its tail.

3. Laying the ears down and baring the teeth.
4. Turning its behind towards the opponent, and
5. Lifting a hind leg.

A horse does not only swish its tail as a threat. A horse that is irritated about something may also swish its tail. Of course, tail swishing is also used to get rid of biting insects.

Social groups

Under natural conditions a herd of horses consists of a number of mares and their foals, possibly also offspring from previous years, plus a stallion. Earlier it was believed that the stallion was the leader of the herd, but studies of horses in the wild have shown that this is not the case. The responsibility of the stallion is to breed the mares, to keep other stallions away, and to defend the herd against predators. Similarly, it was also believed earlier that one of the older and more experienced mares was the actual leader of the group. But again, observations of horses living undisturbed by humans have revealed that, in fact, any member of a group can take the initiative to initiate something such as to go to the watering area. Because of such observations, the concept of leadership (as well as the concepts of dominance and social hierarchies) in groups of horses is questionable.

Although horses are primarily flight animals they are absolutely capable of defending themselves against smaller predators by attacking them. Not only stallions may do so but also mares. Possibly, it is because of this motivation that horses may attack dogs, sheep, or even smaller children. It is important to realize this when, for instance, you want to check the horses in the pasture or if you let the horses share the pasture with sheep and lambs.

Socialization

All behaviour is a mixture of innate and acquired (or learned) behaviour. All behaviour patterns, such as threats or the sucking behaviour of a new-born foal, consist of a basic pattern that is innate and a long series of details that is something that needs to be learned. It is just like the text program on your computer. The basic pattern is programmed on your hard disk but the details, such as what you write, comes from the surroundings (you). A new-born foal has the innate behaviour pattern that makes it search for the udder of the mother. The search under the belly of the mother is innate, just as the smell or the taste of milk probably is. But already after a few attempts the foal learns from where the milk is coming, so that its nursing behaviour becomes much more goal directed and effective.

The same is true of social behaviour. The basic pattern is pre-programmed (for instance threat behaviour or a foal's curiosity towards other foals) but the details must be learned, for instance the meaning of another horse laying back its ears, that it is nice to be groomed on the neck by another horse, etc.

The process a horse goes through to learn to live with other horses is called socialization. It happens optimally while the horse is young, that is, when it is a foal, preferably in groups in which both foals and adults are present.

Intention movements

When horses (and people) think about performing a goal-directed action, the thought process alone (that is, the intention of doing it) will stimulate those nerve cells in the brain that innervate the muscles that will be used for the action. Because of this stimulation the muscles tighten a little and move slightly. In other words, the muscle movements show what the horse (or person) is thinking. This phenomenon, which is called the ideomotoric effect, is the basis for intention movements. Because they occur unconsciously they are 'honest'. They truly show what the horse intends to do.

If a horse that is standing eating out of a bucket is approached by another horse it may want to defend its food by kicking out with a hind leg as the other horse gets nearer. The thought of kicking, that is, the intention of doing so, activates the muscles in the leg and the leg is lifted slightly so that only the front edge of the hoof is touching the ground.

If the approaching horse is properly socialized it will know what the slightly lifted leg means, namely that if it gets too close it will get kicked. The intention movement has become part of the horse's body language. It sends the message 'don't get any closer', that is, it is a threat signal.

If the horse is approached from the front, the thought of defence causes it to flatten its ears (so that they will not get hurt during a fight) and bare its teeth so that they are ready to bite. Both intention movements become part of horses' body language and function as a threat, the latter more strongly than the former.

Body language

Predominantly, horses communicate with each other through body language. Because of that, they are good at reading the body language of other horses. Even the slightest change in the stare of another horse, in the ear position or position of the legs, is noticed.

Horses are not the only ones that communicate their intentions through their body language. We people do too. If we think of performing an action, our thoughts alone will change our body position.

Horses play-fighting

Horses that have regular contact with people also learn our body language. And because they are good at observing the body language of each other, they are also good at observing people's body language.

This is very important to know when working with horses. If we know exactly what we are going to do with our horse in the next few seconds, we communicate through our body language what we intend to do. The horse can read our intention and, therefore, is more inclined to obey. By contrast, if you are unsure about what you want to do, if you for instance hesitate, the horse will notice your uncertainty and be less likely to follow you.

An example is the jumping rider who is fully concentrated on the next jump and who is determined to jump it. The intention of the rider means that she sits in a certain way in the saddle (for instance a little more forward), something that the experienced horse can feel.

In contrast, the jumping rider who hesitates towards a jump may sit in the saddle in a different way (for instance less forward), something that the experienced horse can also feel. In the first case, the horse will be more likely to jump. In the latter case, it will be more likely to refuse the jump.

The more you get to know the body language of the horse, and the better attention you pay to its body language, the better you will be able to predict what the horse will do a second later, and the better you may prepare yourself for its reaction so that you can correct its behaviour the moment it reacts.

Example

You lead your horse home from the pasture. Suddenly, it turns away from you, frees itself, and runs back to the other horses.

But if you pay attention to the horse's body language you will notice that before it turns away from you, it first turns its head slightly, then its neck and front part, and finally its whole body. And when it has turned its neck and shoulder, you have no chance of holding it back.

The whole movement only lasts a fraction of a second, but if you manage to turn its head back towards you, as soon as it starts turning it away, you will be able to stop its flight behaviour and prevent it from running away from you.

> **To learn the body language of horses, and to pay attention to horses' body language, so that you can react slightly before or at the same moment it reacts, is what makes you an experienced and effective rider**

Dominance

Horses living under natural conditions show no sign of dominance but rather try to avoid conflict. Living together in a group is essential for survival. Consequently, cohesion of the group is much more important than dispersal because of some conflict. Of course, a stallion will defend his mares if challenged by another stallion but to say that the winner of such a fight is dominant and higher ranking than the loser is mistaken because this implies a concept of 'rank' that horses do not appear to have. Similarly, a mare threatening another mare that is getting too close to her new-born foal is responding to the actual situation. Her reaction is not affected by some 'social hierarchy' or 'pecking order' idea, simply because she does not have one.

As mentioned above, the concepts of dominance, leadership, and social hierarchy in horses have been formulated mainly because of the way we manage horses. If they are fed 'meals' or kept in stables they may compete at the food trough or defend their territory. And if one particular horse always wins such a fight (because it is bigger or hungrier), it is more correct to assume that it is more aggressive than claiming that it is 'dominant'. The fact that it wins at the food trough does not necessarily mean that it also wins in other conflict situations.

Some horses may respond aggressively (being 'bossy') towards other horses, particularly towards newcomers in a group. In many cases this behaviour is a result of poor socialization earlier in its life. If they have the opportunity, foals and young horses spend a large part of the day interacting not only with their peers but also with adult horses. In nature it is not unusual to see adult stallions interacting with foals. Even though we do not know exactly the function of this interaction, there is little doubt that the young horses learn aspects of the social communication that are so important for life in a social group.

Dominance or leadership when working with horses

Some riders claim that you need to have the top position in the horses' social hierarchy. Even if horses had the mental capability of abstract thinking and formed a social hierarchy, it is very unlikely that they would consider humans part of their social group. Unfortunately, this incorrect but common way of interacting with horses has too often resulted in harsh treatment of them. Of course a horse needs to learn that various signals from the rider or the handler means that it should react in a certain way but the training should be done in a calm, non-aggressive, and 'non-dominating' manner. If done correctly, the horse learns that you are the one who makes the decisions when it is together with you.
Not only does it make work with the horse safer. It also means that it may feel safer when it is together with you.

> **It is very important that your horse learns that it is you who makes the decisions when it is together with you.**

Only if you are the one to decide what your horse is allowed to do and what not, do you have full control over your horse. And only if you have full control over your horse, is it safe to ride.

When you work with a horse you must be sure that

◊   you are the one who decides when it should go forward and when it should stop

◊   you are the one who decides which way it should go

◊   you are the one who decides the gait and the speed

In the section **Training** you can learn how you make your horse obey you so that it fulfils these needs.

In order to teach your horse that it is only allowed to do what it is asked to do, it is important that you give it a clear signal of what you expect it to do (see for instance **Mounting a horse,** page 126).

If, for instance, you are going to lead your horse out of its stable, you should give it a clear signal when to start walking (see **Teaching the horse to go forward,** page 68). It is not allowed to push its way out but should wait quietly until you give it the signal.

To give a clear signal to the horse about what it should do is not something you only do when you train with the horse. It is something that needs to be part of your daily life, that is, also when you just lead your horse out in pasture, when you lead it back from the riding arena, etc.

The fact that you are the one who makes the decisions also means that, as long as you ride your horse or otherwise work with it, it is not allowed to initiate its own behaviour. It is only allowed to do what it has been told to do.

When your horse is together with you, it is only allowed to do what you tell it to do.
        But that means two things:

1.   **that you give it a clear signal**

2.   **that you always make sure that the horse obeys**

When you ride cross country the horse must not be allowed to go and nibble on grass or leaves, to stop up and smell at horse manure, or similar things. That it can do when it is on its own.

In return for your demand for complete obedience, however, you must allow your horse to be a horse. The best way to do so is to let it out into the pasture together with other horses. (See **Horses in the pasture,** page 90)

> **A horse should be allowed to be a horse.**
> **It must have its natural need for social contact fulfilled. It needs to be out in the open together with other horses in a pasture.**
> **If your horse is kept that way, it is in harmony with itself and its environment.**
> **And that makes it safer to ride.**

When horses meet each other

When unfamiliar horses meet they first sniff each other, usually around the mouth and nostrils. When they have done so for a few seconds, one or both of them usually react by vocalising and kicking with a front leg. In rare cases they can also kick out with a hind leg.

When you lead a horse it is safest not to let it get so close to another horse that they can sniff each other. If you allow them to do so, you must not stand right in front of them. You should stay to the side so that you are not hit by a front leg, and nobody should be right behind the horses.

If two horses sniff each other over a fence, there is a risk that they may get a leg into the wire (if it is a wire fence) or caught on a rail (if it is a post-and-rail fence) if they should stamp with a front leg. If two horses in two different enclosures need to meet each other, it is safest to have a low solid wall between them.

Grazing behaviour

Horses are 'continuous eaters' which means that, under natural conditions, they spend a large part of the day grazing. Horses do not eat meals a few times a day.

Grazing consists of the following:

◊ The horse takes one or two steps forward.

◊ Stands still (on average for 12 seconds).

◊ And, on average, it takes eight bites of grass in front and to the sides.

◊ Thereafter, it takes one or two steps again.

◊ The more grass and the longer it is, the longer the time the horse stands still on each spot, and the more bites it may take.

While grazing the horse rarely stands with straight front legs. The front legs are most of the time a little in front or a little behind. In that way the distance down to the grass is less, which means that the horse puts less strain on its back.

The natural grazing behaviour of horses:

◊ Depending upon how much grass is available, and depending upon how fresh it is, under natural conditions horses graze between eight and 18 hours per 24 hours.

◊ If they take a step about every 12 seconds, it means that they take 300 steps an hour or 5,400 steps in 18 hours.

◊ In other words, under natural conditions horses spend a major part of their day and night grazing and moving around in slow walk. During evolution, horses have developed this kind of behaviour and that characteristic has not changed during the domestication of horses.

Feed intake in horses kept individually in a stable:

◊ Riding horses are typically fed two to three times a day with concentrate. It takes about half an hour per meal to eat the food.

◊ In addition, they are given hay or something similar, and most of them are kept on straw. The hay they eat in about three hours. Besides that they may spend a few hours eating straw.

◊ The total time budget is four to eight hours. If the horse is groomed and ridden for two hours a day, and if it sleeps about five hours a night, there is still nine hours per 24 hours in which the horse has nothing to do.

A horse that has been standing unstimulated for a long time in its stable may be more difficult to control during the ride and, consequently, riskier to ride.

An under-stimulated horse is more likely to develop those behaviour patterns called stereotypies, such as weaving, crib biting, or tongue rolling.

Because of the unnatural pattern of locomotion, horses that are standing still for 22–23 hours and are mostly ridden in trot and canter for one to one-and-a-half hours per 24 hours, are more susceptible to damage in legs and joints.

The best way to stimulate a horse is to let it out in pasture every day. Fat horses should preferably be kept in pasture that has already been grazed by other animals (such as cattle, sheep or other horses), so that they need to 'work' more, that is walk more for their food. And if there is no grass at all, a supplement of hay or haylage can be given.

Horses that are in pasture together with other horses move around more than horses kept alone in a pasture. Therefore, horses should be together with other horses when they get out in pasture.

Horses that for some reason need to be kept indoors can be stimulated to some degree if they can watch other horses, for instance through an open window.

> **The more a horse has its natural need for stimulation fulfilled (which for horses especially means grazing) and the more it has its need for social contact fulfilled, the more the horse lives in harmony with itself and its environment and the safer it is to ride and to handle**

Resting behaviour

Even though horses under natural conditions spend a lot of time grazing, going to the watering place, and doing other activities, they also need to rest. Horses can rest while standing up and while lying down. They only lie down for a few hours, mostly during the night. All horses lie down at least once during the 24-hour period, also old horses. Part of their sleep can be obtained standing up, but the dream sleep (also called REM-sleep) they can only obtain when they lie down.

Most of the time they lie on their chest with their head and neck kept up or, possibly, resting their head on the ground. But once in a while, they lie flat out on their side. In this position they sleep their dream sleep. Sometimes you can notice their legs move, just like dogs sometimes do when they dream.

The lying and sleeping pattern of horses (approximately)

◊ Horses stand up for 22 hours.

◊ They lie down for two hours.

◊ They are awake for 19 hours.

◊   They doze for two hours.

◊   They sleep for three hours, one of these in dream sleep.

Foals and young horses have a greater need for lying down. Foals especially have many lying down phases throughout the day and night.

Horses that are stabled in unfamiliar surroundings often hesitate to lie down. The first night they may not lie down at all and during the following nights only for a short time. The same thing may happen in the early summer when horses are turned out in pasture day and night.

Horses that are being transported do not lie down. Foals will lie down during transport. Some horses have problems lying down (and getting up) in small spaces.

It is important that horses get enough rest. The more work we demand of them (during training, riding, cross country riding, competitions), the more and the longer breaks they need.

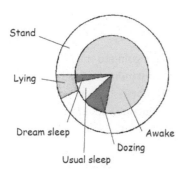

Chapter 3

Pasture

WHY IS IT IMPORTANT THAT HORSES ARE LET OUT IN PASTURE?

As mentioned above about natural behaviour, horses are pronounced herd animals that feel safest when they are together with other horses. Although not all horses perform mutual grooming behaviour, they may still prefer to graze or stand and rest near other horses, indicating that they feel safer than being alone.

Scientific studies on young horses have shown that their need for contact with other horses cannot be satisfied if there is a wall between the horses. Their need for social contact is only satisfied completely if they have the opportunity for physical contact.

Studies have also shown that horses that are kept together with other horses are easier to handle and to work with. In addition, horses that stimulate each other are less likely to react to sounds and movements and more likely to remain calm.

In order for horses to be outdoors in a social group without accidents occurring, two things are of importance

◊ First of all, it is necessary that the horses (preferably while they are foals) have learned to be together with other horses. The social language (see **Socialization,** page 40) is not only innate but also something that needs to be learned.

◊ Secondly, the people who take care of the horses need much more knowledge of, and experience with, horses, when they are kept loose in a pasture.

The most important safety aspects in connection with bringing a horse out to pasture or home are described under **Horses in the pasture,** page 90.

Horses that are loose, either in a pasture, in a stable, or any other place, always constitute a risk. When you approach horses that are loose you always need to keep an eye on them, not only the horse you want to get hold of but also the other horses nearby. Each one of them will be able to kick out and hit you, either because they get scared of something, because they want to play, or because they are aggressive, for instance towards the horse you catch.

In that kind of situations, you must never turn your back to the horses before you are sufficiently far away from them so that they cannot reach you with a kick.

Always keep an eye on horses that are loose, as long as you are near them. Never turn your back to them before you are far enough away from them

The four most important reasons for letting out horses in pasture every day are:

1. Horses have a need for physical contact with other horses
2. Horses need fresh air
3. Horses need to walk or run around
4. Horses need to roll

1. Horses have a need for physical contact with other horses.

As described under Horse behaviour horses feel safer when they are together with other horses. For many horses it is not enough only to see, hear and smell other horses, for instance in a neighbouring stable. They also need to be able to touch each other, to groom each other, to graze next to each other, or just to stand and rest near each other.

Especially for young horses, it is important to be together with other horses so that they have the opportunity to play with each other. Through play, they learn the social language that is so important for living together peacefully.

The function of play is partly that horses learn social communication, and partly that they get the opportunity to develop friendships. Besides, the fact that they move around more in a social group has a beneficial effect on their development.

2. Horses need fresh air.

No matter how good the air is in the stable, it is better outside. The lungs of a horse are able to obtain a lot of oxygen which it needs for running. But the respiratory system of horses is also sensitive to dust and ammonia, which is plentiful in any stable. That is why it is important that they get fresh air in their lungs every day, including when it is cold. The daily stay outdoors strengthens their immune defence and renders them less susceptible to colds and influenza. Only if it is raining or very windy is it better that the horses have shelter or are stabled.

3. Horses need to walk or run around.

In nature, horses walk for up to18 hours a day and take up to 5,400 steps per 24 hours (see **Grazing behaviour,** page 45).

The legs and joints of horses are developed for many hours' daily locomotion. During locomotion the blood circulation to bones, joints and muscles is stimulated which strengthens them. A horse that moves around several hours a day in a paddock or in a pasture, either when it grazes or follows other horses around, is less likely to become lame or to suffer damage than a horse standing still all day in a stable.

4.   Horses need to roll.

We do not quite know why horses roll. But there is little doubt that it is important for them to do so, otherwise they would not do it. Horses that are wet from sweat or rain like to roll in sand or dry dirt. Horses irritated by insects like to roll in mud.

Although it means extra work to brush a dusty or muddy horse, it is important to give them the opportunity to roll. But it means that they are allowed to do so without a blanket.

Only if it rains or is very windy and there is no opportunity to seek shelter, should you put a rug on a horse. It makes no sense to let it stand and freeze in the paddock.

A good way to get to know your horse is to observe it while it is in pasture together with other horses. So sit down some place where the horses do not notice you and spend a couple of hours watching how your horse spends its time. Notice if it keeps close to another horse, if it plays with certain horses, or grooms and is groomed by certain other horses.

In this way you may see which other horses are its friends (or enemies) and how important it is for your horse to be able to rest, to graze, to play, and whatever horses spend their time doing.

Fence

As important it is to let horses out in pasture, it is just as important to make sure that they stay in the pasture. There are two ways to do so. One way is to use a kind of fence that the horses respect. Either it has to be so solid that they cannot rub it apart or push their way through it, or they have to be kept away by an electric wire. Since electric fences are usually not solid, they have to be checked regularly. Is the wire hanging isolated on the fence posts? Are weeds and other growth removed from the wire? Is the wire actually 'hot' (electrified)? (If you do not have a wire tester at hand, pick a long grass straw, hold it in one end, and touch the wire with the other end. The closer you move your hand towards the wire, the more strongly you will be able to feel the electric current without it hurting you).

The other way to ensure that the horses stay in the pasture is to make sure that they have what they need in terms of water, something to munch on (grass, haylage, straw, bark from cut off branches, or something similar), plus the company of some friendly horses. The more the horses like the pasture, the smaller is the risk that they will try to break out. (See also **Catching horses that have escaped from their pasture,** page 98).

Chapter 4

Training the horse to be safe

IN order to be able to work with and, particularly, to ride on a horse in a safe way, it is important

◊   that you are good at riding

◊   that you know how horses react

◊   that you are able to train your horse

◊   that you know some of the dangerous situations that can happen.

How you train your horse and how you habituate it to some of the situations that we know can frighten a horse is described in this chapter.

Apart from becoming a good rider you must train your horse so that it is well behaved and that it continues to be well behaved.

As long as your horse is together with you it must obey you. You are the one who makes the decisions. Only if you have full control over your horse is it safe to ride and to handle. But to obey a person is something that the horse must learn. It is not an innate characteristic. Good behaviour is something that has to be learned.

To teach your horse to be well behaved is something you do when you train your horse. But it is not just young horses that must learn new things while they are being started. Also older horses must be trained, especially if they have developed bad habits.

Professional help

For children and young riders it may be difficult to handle a horse. For grown-ups it may be difficult to handle a somewhat wild horse. In both cases it may be necessary to involve the help of a more experienced person to help with the training so that the horse learns correct behaviour in the right way.

It is important that you know your limits as a rider. Remember, the fact that you cannot handle a horse that has some kind of a problem does not necessarily mean that you are not a good rider.

> **REMEMBER:**
> **If you have a problem with your horse,**
> **get help from a more experienced rider.**

But it is just as important to realize that it is not enough that the horse learns the right behaviour when the person helping you is doing the training. It is just as important that it learns the right behaviour when *you* work with it. The way to reach that goal is to let the more experienced person (the instructor) start the training. Thereafter, you continue with the training, while the instructor is watching, so that he or she can still intervene, if necessary. In other words, the transition from having the instructor work with the horse to having you do the work must be gradual, so that the horse learns to behave also when you are doing the work.

> **It is not good enough that the riding instructor can make the horse react correctly. The rider of the horse must also be able to make the horse respond correctly.**

The chapter consists of four parts:

◊ Conditions around training

◊ Learning

◊ Basic training

◊ Applied training

The importance of habits, where, how much, and how often you should train, how to use reward and punishment, and what kind of equipment you need, is described in the section **Conditions around training (this page)**.

The methods that we use when we teach a horse to behave is described in the section **Learning**, page 59.

How you teach your horse to stop, to go forward etc., both when you lead it and when you ride it, is described in the section **Basic training**, page 68.

How you use the training methods to teach your horse to accept different situations that often create problems is described in the section **Applied training**, page 74.

CONDITIONS AROUND TRAINING

Obedience training

In order to work with and to ride your horse in a safe way you need to teach it to show certain behaviours in certain situations. The way you teach it to do so is described later in this section. It is important that you train the different exercises with your horse. But it is just as important that you insist on your horse showing the correct behaviour not only when you train. The horse must also show correct behaviour during the daily work.

This means that you have to establish a habit of always insisting on your horse showing the right behaviour. For instance, every time you mount your horse it must stand still (see **Mounting a horse, page 126**). Every time you ride, indoors or outside, it must obey your signals to go forward, stop, etc. If you teach your horse these good habits from the very beginning, you will have a horse that is safe to ride.

It is important to be consistent and to demand correct behaviour, particularly in the beginning of the training. Even if it means that you have to be a little more patient and even though it may take a little more time, remember that the time and effort you invest in the beginning, you will get back later on, when the horse has learned correct behaviour.

Habits

Horses are animals of pronounced habits that function best when they do the same things in specific situations. For instance, if a horse learns from day one that it must stand still when you mount it, it will always stand still in that situation.

But it means that, from the very beginning, you absolutely must demand that it stands still every time you mount it. If it takes one step forward while you have one foot in the stirrup, you must take the foot out again and make the horse go back one step, before you again put your foot in the stirrup. If your horse shall learn to stand still when you mount it, even one small step forward constitutes disobedience. Maybe you have to repeat the correction five times or more on the first day, before the horse stands still. But already next time you mount it, it may only take three corrections before it stands still. And next time two corrections, etc. before it has learned it.

Apart from establishing good habits from the very beginning, it is important to realize that, once in a while, many horses will test if the rules are still valid or if they have been changed. This means that, after a while when your horse has been standing still while you mount it, suddenly it tries to take a step forward. If you correct its behaviour at once, it will again stand still when you mount it in the future. But if you do not correct its behaviour, it will be very quick to develop a new habit, namely to go forward while you mount it. That is the reason why it is not enough to train a horse while it is young or while you start riding it. Training and maintenance of good behaviour is something that continues all the time. The habits must be maintained.

Obviously, it is much easier to establish good habits in young horses that have not, already, established habits. For that reason it is important that young horses are trained by experienced trainers. It is much more difficult to establish good habits in horses that have already developed bad habits. A horse that for years has been used to going ahead as soon as the rider puts a foot in the stirrup will need much more training, before it learns to stand still. And in the beginning, it will test the rule much more often to see if it can return to the old habit.

If you share the horse with other riders and you are the only one who trains good habits, obviously, it is much more difficult to get a well behaved horse. But it is not impossible. There is nothing wrong in demanding that the horse stands still when you mount it, even though the other riders do not demand it. A horse is able to learn how to behave under one rider, and not necessarily be well behaved under another rider. But because it necessitates much more training, the best solution is, of course, that both or all riders ask the same and agree on the training.

Horses are pronounced animals of habits. To follow a daily pattern makes them feel safe. To change the daily pattern makes them insecure.

◊   If a horse is always taken out of its stable in the same way, always groomed and saddled in the same place, and always ridden after the same programme, for instance by the same person, a change in the routine alone may make it insecure if, for instance, suddenly another person does the job.

◊   If you always tie up the horse a certain place to groom it, doing it another place may be reason enough that it suddenly pulls back or refuses to stand still.

◊   And if you always ride a certain stretch of the daily ride in canter, the horse will soon learn to canter when it arrives at that place. If the horse is ridden by the usual person, it may be all right. But if the horse one day is ridden by another rider who does not know the routine, the sudden canter may come as an unpleasant surprise.

To avoid this kind of habit formation, it is necessary once in a while to vary the routines. This means that you should groom and saddle the horse in different places and that you ride the 'canter place' sometimes in canter, other times in walk and trot.

Riding school horses especially have to get used to the fact that things are done in different ways, because many different riders should be able to handle them. In other words, if you want a flexible horse you need to change routines frequently.

Reward

> **The training of your horse should be done so that you reward its correct behaviour and you prevent it from showing incorrect behaviour.**

The more you follow this principle, the better your horse will keep its motivation to learn. On the contrary, if you only ignore your horse when it does something right, and punish it when it does something wrong, the training gets to be a negative experience for the horse. It loses its motivation to learn.

The best way to teach your horse correct behaviour is to reward it when it shows the wanted behaviour. There are different kinds of reward.

The most effective reward is to release the pressure you used to tell it what it should do, as described later. The main reason why it is effective is that it is given at the same moment the horse shows the correct behaviour. (This type of reward is called negative reinforcement, as described later.) Some people do not consider release of pressure a reward. If the release is given immediately after (or maybe even during) the correct response, it tells the horse very effectively that it showed the correct response. But of course, the release may not have the same positive aspect as a positive reinforcement.

If you want to add a positive element to the training and tell the horse that what it just did was good, pat it on the side of the neck or on the withers. A stroke is better than a slap. To scratch the horse on the withers, right in front of the saddle, has a calming effect. If you at the same time say 'good boy' or something similar, the horse learns (through associative learning) that your words are also a reward. Combining the release of pressure (the negative reinforcement) with a stroke on the withers (a positive reinforcement) will make the training more positive for the horse and enhance its motivation to learn.

Horse trainers disagree on whether you should use treats as a reward when training horses. The advantage with treats is that they motivate the horse which makes the training more effective. The disadvantage is, however, that they may make the horse beg or possibly bite. In order for a treat to facilitate learning, it must be given the very moment that the horse shows the correct behaviour. Only then does it work as a reward and only then does it motivate the horse to show the behaviour more often. If the treat is given after that the horse has shown a different behaviour (for instance, after it has scraped with a front hoof or after it has bitten you to get the treat), the wrong kind of behaviour is rewarded.

If you give the treat intermittently (that means not every time the horse shows the correct behaviour but only sometimes) the horse will be more likely to show the correct behaviour. Using the rewards variably, sometimes giving a treat, sometimes a stroke on the withers, and sometimes praise, the horse will not know what kind of reward to expect and at the same time learn that it is all a reward.

When you give your horse a treat, hold your palm out flat so that it does not bite your fingers.

(See a good example on how useful treats can be in the section **Habituating your horse to plastic**, page 79. See also how a break during the ride can be a reward in the section **Riding with loose reins**, page 129.)

Punishment

The only effect of punishment is to show the horse that the behaviour response it showed right before it was punished was wrong. A punishment does not show the horse what the correct response is. If you punish a horse for something it did, do not expect that it will show the correct response afterwards.

If, for instance, the horse bites or kicks, punishment may have an effect. The punishment may make it less likely that it will bite or kick in the future.

If you try to teach your horse a new behaviour response, for instance to stand still when you approach it, obviously it will be wrong to punish it if it does not stand still.

If you are not absolutely sure that your horse is disobedient, you should not punish it. If the horse is disobedient because it is scared or because it does not understand what you want, punishment will only make it more scared or more uncertain. In that case it is better to ignore the horse's behaviour and to repeat the signal in a clearer way.

If you must punish the horse, do it as mildly as possible. The purpose of punishment is to convey to the horse that the behaviour it just showed was wrong. The purpose is not to cause pain. If the horse reacts to being yelled at, that may be punishment enough to correct its behaviour.

> **To punish a horse that does not obey because it does not understand what the rider wants does not improve the horse's understanding.**
> **On the contrary.**

Whip

As described later, you should use a whip when you train your horse. But you should only use it for tapping. The tapping should only irritate the horse. It should not hurt. And as soon as the horse responds just a little bit correctly (and for instance takes just half a step forward), you must stop the tapping. (See also **Negative reinforcement,** page 63).

It is a good idea to touch the horse with the whip on different parts of the body (neck, back, legs). If the horse is afraid of the whip, it is because you or somebody else has used the whip too harshly. In that case, you have to habituate the horse to the whip. Show the horse the whip and let it sniff it. Scratch it with the handle of the whip on a place where it likes to be scratched. If the horse tries to avoid the whip, try not to remove the whip before the horse has calmed down.

Timing

Timing means to do the right thing at the right moment.

The most important aspect of both reward and punishment is that it is given at the very moment that the horse shows the correct (or the wrong) reaction. As soon as it takes a step forward as a response to leg pressure, you must reward it by releasing the pressure. If you think that it is necessary to punish the horse, you must punish it the very moment it shows the unwanted behaviour. If there is a time lag of just a few seconds between behaviour and reward/punishment, the horse does not understand the connection and the reward or punishment has no effect.

Equipment

◊   When you train your horse from the ground, it should wear a halter or bridle

◊   When you train from the saddle, your horse should wear a bridle

◊   To help the training, you should use a long whip

◊   Other equipment (spurs, draw reins, etc.) should only be used by experienced riders and only for horses that have specific problems because of incorrect training

Where should you train?

◊   In principle, you can train anywhere. Most important is that your horse is calm and is not distracted by other activities nearby.

◊   If your horse remains calm when it is separated from other horses, it is best to train it when it is alone. Then it is easier for the horse to concentrate on the training.

◊   If your horse gets nervous when it is separated from other horses, it is best to start the training with another (calm) horse nearby. Of course, later it still needs to learn to obey also when it is alone.

◊   In the beginning it may be advantageous to train in an indoor arena. The less that is going on around the horse, the better it can concentrate on the training.

◊   Later you should also train when other horses are present, as well as outdoors. Your horse must learn to obey under all conditions.

◊   If you do not have access to an indoor arena, you should start the training where the horse 'feels home'.

How much should you train?

◊   You only have to train a couple of times every week. The breaks between the training sessions help the horse remember what it has learned. But of course, it takes longer to get through all the training than if you train every day.

◊   You should only train 15–20 minutes every time. Do not train for too long a time. Your horse is not able to concentrate longer than that. And if it cannot concentrate on the training, it will not learn anything.

◊   In general it is a good idea to vary the training, so that new exercises follow something the horse has learned earlier, possibly followed by a relaxing ride in the countryside. In that way you maintain the motivation of the horse and its willingness to work.

LEARNING

Both under natural conditions and in relation to training, horses learn according to certain principles. As shown in the previous picture horses learn a lot by observing other horses, for instance the foal that copies its mother.

But horses also learn in other ways and it is the principles of these other ways that we use when we train horses. The three most important principles are:

◊ Learning through habituation

◊ Learning through reinforcement

◊ Learning through association

Learning through reinforcement is also called operant conditioning.
Learning through association is also called classical conditioning.

Habituation

If an animal is repeatedly exposed to a certain stimulation that has neither a positive nor a negative consequence, it will gradually cease to respond to the stimulation.

◊ Example. A horse is exposed to a loud sound. It may react by flinching and running forwards five steps. If the sound is repeated shortly afterwards, the horse again flinches and runs forward three steps. After several repetitions the horse reacts less and less, until it finally remains standing without reacting to the sound.

If the whole situation is repeated a few days later, the horse may again react to the sound, possibly a little bit less than the first time. In addition, it usually takes fewer repetitions before it stops reacting to the sound. After sufficient repetitions, the horse learns that the sound is not dangerous.

Young horses in a paddock near a road may run off when a vehicle drives by. When it has happened sufficient times, they cease to react. If the young horses are together with older, experienced horses that do not react to the traffic, the younger ones will habituate to the traffic faster. The older horses will have a calming effect on the young horses.

If one of the young horses is led out of the paddock where it has habituated to the traffic, it may still be frightened by a car driving by, either because the car is closer to the horse or because it happens in a new place. Usually, however, the horse will react less intensely and habituate to cars on the road faster, compared to horses that have not been kept in the paddock.

The habituation that takes place in the paddock is not necessarily a guarantee that the horse does not react outside the paddock. It may still be necessary to train outside the paddock, for instance on the shoulder of a less busy road (see also **Habituating the horse to tractors,** page 77, and **Habituating the horse to motor cycles,** page 78).

A horse can get scared of many things and situations. It is impossible to habituate it to everything. Therefore, it is necessary to think about those things and situations that you are most likely to encounter when you ride your horse. If you live in a suburban area you should habituate your horse to cars, trucks, motorcycles etc. If you live in the countryside you should habituate it to tractors, harvesters etc. (See **Applied training,** page 74).

Since it is much easier to habituate a horse to something BEFORE it has developed fear of it, it is a good idea to train it in those situations mentioned later. Not only does it mean less training, but it also means that you can avoid some dangerous situations. In addition, you get to know your horse much better. You will find out how it reacts when it is exposed to something new and unknown. And last but not least, your horse will learn to feel safe in your company. It will learn to trust you.

Habituation methods

The first time a horse is exposed to something that may scare it, the stimulus can be given at full intensity. For instance, if you want to habituate your horse to plastic bags blowing in the wind, you can wave the bag in the air close to the horse, until it calms down. This approach is called 'flooding'

Using the flooding method may not be the best approach because there is a risk that you get the opposite result, that the horse ends up being more scared of plastic bags. Another disadvantage is that the horse may react so strongly that it causes an accident.

Another approach to habituate a horse is to expose it to the stimulus in a much gentler way. Instead of waving the plastic bag close to the horse, you first let it sniff the bag without waving it. Then you go some distance away from the horse (or have a helper do it) and wave the bag. You need to go so far away that the horse remains reasonably calm. Thereafter, you gradually move closer to the horse while waving the bag. But do not approach too fast. The horse should still remain reasonably calm. This approach is called habituation by successive approximation. The advantage is that you decide yourself how much or how little you want to scare the horse. In that way it is easier to avoid an accident. Another is that the chance that the horse ends up less scared of plastic bags is greater. (See also **Habituating your horse to plastic,** page 79.)

One example of habituation using flooding or successive approximation is the way a horse is started (that is, learning to carry a saddle and rider).

The 'cowboy method' is to put a saddle and a bridle on the inexperienced horse, to sit up on it, and to let it buck until it calms down, at which point the rider starts to ride it. This approach is similar to the flooding method.

Another approach is, first, to habituate the horse to having a girth around its chest, then to have a blanket on its back, then a saddle and more and more weight, until the rider can finally sit on its back and the actual riding lessons can begin. This approach, which may last several training sessions, is habituation by successive approximation. (See also **Starting a young horse,** page 80)

> **The best way to habituate your horse to something that it is afraid of is to expose it to the object or situation with so low an intensity that it only gets slightly scared, and thereafter to repeat the exposure with gradually increasing intensity.**

The way you can habituate your horse to a place that it is scared of:

1. Lead or ride the horse forward and stop sufficiently far from the place that the horse remains reasonably calm.
2. Repeat the exercise and go a metre (or more) closer.
3. Repeat until you are all the way past the place.

If space allows it an alternative way is to ride by in a half circle, turn around and ride back also in a half circle, and to repeat riding back and forth while making the circle smaller (see **Riding past scary things,** page 147).

If you are afraid that the horse may react too strongly (and, for instance rear), you can start by leading it. But later when it has learned to remain calm, you must repeat the habituation when you ride it.

Habituation is the simplest form of learning. Horses habituate to numerous things without us noticing. For instance, they habituate to the many different kinds of pressure. Pressure from the saddle girth, the bit in its mouth, from blankets, etc. If your horse is used to you riding with a jacket on and one day you have a rain coat on, the sound or the touch of the rain coat on its back can frighten it, until it has gotten used to it.

Sometimes we notice that the horse reacts a little to something new, but often we do not notice it.

Most horses habituate relatively fast to new and unknown things and situations. They also habituate relatively fast to different kinds of pressure. But there are two kinds of pressure that we do not want them to get used to. One kind is the pressure we use to make them go forward (pressure from the legs), the other is the pressure we use to stop them (pressure from the bit).

To avoid this kind of habituation, it is important ALWAYS (that is, every time) to demand that the horse reacts correctly when we use these kinds of pressure. If we press with our legs without getting the correct reaction (that the horse goes forward), the horse habituates to leg pressure and, thus, learns not to obey.

How you avoid your horse habituating to leg pressure and pressure from the bit is described in the section **Basic training,** page 68,

See also examples on habituation in the section **Applied training,** page 74.

Generalization

It is a common experience to habituate a horse to something, such as a jacket hanging over the railing of the riding arena and then shortly afterwards experience how the horse gets scared of the same jacket just because it is hanging a different place. Or you habituate your horse to a red tractor but it still gets scared of a blue tractor. It is very tempting to conclude that the horse is not very bright. Some riders may even lose their patience and punish the horse.

To conclude that the jacket hanging the second place is not dangerous because the same jacket was not dangerous the first place, or to conclude that the blue tractor is not dangerous because the red one was not, is called generalization. Horses are not good at this. In fact, under natural conditions there is a better chance of staying alive by not generalizing. Just because a big stone to the left is not dangerous, there may still be a predator hiding behind the stone to the right.

The consequence of horses' lack of generalization is that we need to habituate them to as many different things as possible, and we need to do the training in as many different places as possible. Do not only train in the indoor arena and expect that what the horse learned there, it also knows outside.

Overshadowing

Overshadowing means that, if an animal is exposed to two mutually exclusive signals at the same time, it will react to the signal that is strongest. If, for instance, you train with your horse and it is suddenly frightened by a loud sound, it will react to the sound and ignore your signal. The sound affects the horse more than your signal.

But overshadowing can also be used in connection with habituation. When you habituate your horse to something that scares it, you can divert its attention somewhat from the scary thing. While the horse is exposed to the scary stimulation, you can practice some of the exercises described later (see **Basic training,** page 68), such as to stop the horse, to let it step back, or similar things. The more the horse focuses on the signals from the trainer, the less focus it will have on the scary things.

Learning through reinforcement

(also called learning through trial-and-error)

If an animal tries a certain behaviour that results in something that feels good for the animal, it will show the behaviour more often.

> Example 1. If a horse tries to open the lid of the food box and it succeeds, it will try to open the box more often. Eating the food in the box is a reward for the horse's behaviour to open the box. The reward is called a positive reinforcer; reinforcer because the behaviour 'to open the box' is shown more often, and positive because something is added (that is, the food).

> Example 2. If a horse feels a branch pressing on its leg, it will lift the leg to avoid the pressure. The behaviour of the horse, to lift the leg, makes the horse feel better, because the pressure is removed. The release of the pressure is called a negative reinforcer; reinforcer because the

behaviour 'to lift the leg' is shown every time there is a pressure, and negative because something is removed (that is, the pressure from the branch).

The two examples demonstrate that there are two kinds of reinforcement or reward.

◊   Positive reinforcement: the horse is in a 'normal' state and obtains something that increases its feeling of pleasure (such as the food).

◊   Negative reinforcement: the horse is in a somewhat unpleasant state (something that presses) and succeeds in getting back to a 'normal' state (removal of the pressure).

When we train horses we use both kinds of reinforcements. The positive reinforcement we use when we praise the horse or pat it on the neck. The negative reinforcement (release of pressure) we use when we make the horse go forward, stop, yield, or go backwards.

Negative reinforcement

Negative reinforcement is the most important kind of reinforcement that we use when working with horses. In fact, the moment you put on a halter or a bridle on the horse, you make preparation to use negative reinforcement. To make the horse go forward when leading from the ground you put a slight tension on lead rope or reins forward. The tension creates a pressure from the neck piece of the halter or the bridle on the horse's neck. To avoid the pressure the horse steps forward. On a well-trained horse the pressure is so little that it is more correct to call it a signal.

As soon as the horse takes one step forward you must reinforce it for showing the right behaviour by releasing the pressure. In that way, the horse learns that a light pressure in the neck means that it must go forward.

It is the same principle when you ride the horse. A light pressure with your legs on the sides of the horse will make it go forward. As soon as it responds in the right way, you must release the leg pressure.

If the horse does not respond, you can increase the pressure either by pressing harder with your heels or by tapping lightly several times with your heels. If the horse still does not respond you can tap with your whip right behind your leg (see **Whip,** page 57).

The very moment the horse responds correctly you must stop your pressure, both with your legs and with the whip tapping. Remember that it is the release from pressure that is the reinforcement . And it is the reinforcement that makes the horse respond correctly next time you give a light pressure.

To stop the horse you exert light tension on the lead rope or the reins. The tension creates pressure on the nose from the halter, or pressure on the lower jaw from the bit. To avoid the pressure the horse stops. As soon as the horse has stopped, you must reinforce the correct behaviour by releasing the pressure. In that way, the horse learns that a light pressure on the nose or on the jaw means that it should stop.

If the horse does not understand the meaning of the light pressure, either because it has never learned or because it has got away with not responding correctly, you must not only continue but also increase the pressure, until the horse shows the right reaction.

The right way to use negative reinforcement during initial training of your horse is:

1. To give a light pressure.
2. To give a stronger pressure if the light one has no effect.
3. To release the pressure.

The first pressure is the signal to the horse of what it should do (the pressure in the neck from the halter or on its sides from your legs means to go forward; the pressure on the nose or jaw means to stop).

If the horse does not respond on the first signal a more intense and uncomfortable pressure follows until the horse responds.

The release of the pressure is the reinforcement that tells the horse that it has responded correctly.

The more you make the first light pressure be the signal that makes the horse respond and the better you are at releasing the pressure as soon as the horse has responded correctly, the more sensitive your horse will be. The horse must learn (through association, as described later) to react to the first light pressure in order to avoid the following more intense pressure.

But you will only get a sensitive horse if you release the pressure at the right moment.

> **The pressure stimulates**
> **The release of the pressure motivates**

The pressure should make the horse respond. If it does not respond to the intense pressure, you need the help of the whip. You use the whip by tapping repeatedly until the horse responds. You should not tap or hit harder than you are able to hit yourself without it hurting.

> **The whip tapping should irritate the horse.**
> **It should not hurt the horse.**

Training by ignoring a behaviour

A horse can also learn from the fact that a reinforcement or a reward does not follow.

Example: You lunge your horse. Then you call it and pull on the lunge line until the horse comes up to you. When it arrives you give it a piece of carrot. When you have repeated it a few times the horse learns to connect its approach with a piece of carrot.

The horse may now start to come up to you, whether you call it or not, simply because it wants a piece of carrot. If you give it the carrot it has learned that it gets a reward when it comes up to you. It has not learned to come when you call it.

In contrast, if you ignore the horse when it comes to you without you calling, and you only give it a carrot when it comes to you after you have called it, it will learn that it only gets the reward when it obeys your call.

Not giving it a carrot when it comes without you calling it, is called extinction. The horse learns that coming without the call does not result in a reward. So ignoring the horse has taught it only to come when you call it.

Many bad habits can be treated in the same way. If, for instance, your horse begs by 'pawing' with a front leg to get a treat, the best thing you can do is to ignore it. Just go away from it. That is much more effective than yelling at it.

Signals

The purpose of training your horse is to teach it to react in a certain way when you give it a certain signal.

Many behaviour problems in horses develop because they receive opposite signals or signals they do not understand.

◊   You should use one signal to make the horse go forward (a slight tension forward on the lead rope or a light pressure with the legs).

◊   You should use another signal to make it stop (a slight tension on lead rope or reins).

◊   You make the horse turn by giving a light tension on the lead rope or reins in the direction you want it to turn.

> **It is very important that a specific signal is only used to make the horse show one specific reaction.**

A specific signal must only be used for one specific reaction. A signal must not mean that sometimes the horse should do one thing and other times it should do another thing. This will confuse the horse and cause a conflict situation. As mentioned in the section **Collecting a horse,** page 131, a signal must only result in one kind of behaviour. Tension on the reins means stop. Tension on the reins must not be used to get the horse to go in a certain head and neck position. In contrast, there is nothing wrong in using several different signals to get the same behaviour. A horse has no problem learning to go forward after leg pressure as well as a pull forward on the lead rope.

Primary versus secondary signals

The signals you give with the lead rope, reins, or legs are called primary signals. Some riders teach their horse to go forward and to stop when they say 'walk' and 'stop'. These signals are called secondary signals. There is nothing wrong in teaching your horse to respond to secondary signals, as long as you also teach them the meaning of the primary signals. The main reason for this is that primary signals you can intensify; secondary signals you cannot intensify. If your horse charges because it is frightened, you can pull harder on the reins. If your horse had only learned to stop for your voice command, yelling 'stop' several times or yelling louder would not have much effect. Similarly, if you train trailer loading and your horse refuses to go forward, pulling harder and using whip tapping will eventually make your horse go forward. Yelling 'walk' louder would have no effect.

Once the horse has learned to respond correctly to the primary signals it is a good idea also to teach it secondary signals. If a horse has learned to stop both from the pressure of the halter or bit and for the command 'stop', you do not have to have physical contact with the horse to stop it (see example under **Teaching a horse to stop when the rider has fallen off**, page 133).

Learning through association

If an animal experiences a certain situation at the same time something else happens, it may connect the two happenings with each other.

If the animal experiences the situation at a certain place, it may connect the location with the happening.

> Example 1. If you give your horse feed from a feed wagon, it will soon connect the sound of the wagon with food.

> Example 2. If a horse experiences something unpleasant from a certain person (for instance a veterinarian, a blacksmith), it will be afraid of the person next time they meet.

> Example 3. If a horse is exposed to something frightening at a certain place, in the future it will be afraid of approaching the place.

Learning through association is a learning method that we also use to our advantage. If we make the wire that surrounds the paddock electric, the horse will learn to connect the discomfort of the electric shock with the wire, with the location of the wire, or with both wire and location.

When the horse has done something right, we reward it, for instance by stroking its neck. If we say 'good boy' at the same time, the horse will learn that the sound 'good boy' also is a reward.

If we combine a reward with a special sound (such as the click from a toy frog), the horse will learn that the click is also a reward. That is the principle we use in clicker training.

The most important example on learning through association is what happens (or should happen) in connection with negative reinforcement, as described under **Learning through reinforcement**, page 59.

In the beginning the training consists of:

1. giving a light pressure as a signal to react
2. giving a more intense pressure that is unpleasant for the horse and that makes it react

3. releasing the pressure as a reinforcement for reacting correctly.

Through repeated training the horse will learn (through association) the connection between the stronger unpleasant pressure and the light pressure, so that it reacts on the light pressure alone to avoid the stronger pressure.

> **When the horse has learned the connection between the intense and the light pressure, it is possible to control it by means of the light pressure (that is the signal) alone. The horse is thus sensitive to the aids.**

Learning through association can also be used later in the training. If you encourage the forward movement of the horse with your seat by tightening the abdominal and lower back muscles at the same time that you press with your legs, it will learn to increase the speed when you give the signal with your seat alone. But it is important first to teach the horse to react to the light leg pressure and, when it does so, then to teach it to react to the seat.

The horse can also learn other associations during riding. If you lean back a little at the same time as you put tension on the reins to slow down the horse, it will learn to slow down when you lean back. If you put a little more weight on one seat bone at the same time as you open the rein slightly by turning your hand so the thumb points out to the same side, the horse will learn to turn to the side from the weight alone.

This kind of learning actually happens even if we are not aware of it. For instance, when we think of making a certain movement, our thought alone will make our body move slightly. The connection between our thought (or intention) and our small movement is the basis for our body language (see **Intention movements,** page 41 and **Body language,** p.41). If for instance we think of picking up something lying on a table in front of us, the thought alone will make our hand move slightly towards the table.

As described in the section **The behaviour of the horse in relation to safety** (page 30), horses are good at reading each other's body language. Horses that are in close contact with people learn to read our body language. That is why a horse often knows what we are going to do the very moment that we think of doing it. And this happens whether we walk next to the horse or sit on its back.

A Swedish experiment has shown that the nervousness of the rider can spread to the horse so that it, too, gets nervous. Both horses and riders in the experiment were equipped with heart rate monitors. Before they were asked to ride around in an indoor arena, each rider was told that, when they came to a certain point in the hall, an umbrella would be opened in order to test the fear reaction of the horse. When horse and rider came to the designated point, the umbrella was not opened, however, but still the heart rate went up, both in the rider and in the horse. The rider expected something to happen, whereas the horse reacted to the tension of the rider,

Counter-conditioning

In practical situations the different learning principles are often combined to improve learning. One way is to use counter conditioning which means substituting an undesirable behaviour with a desirable behaviour that is incompatible with the undesirable behaviour.

If, for instance, you want to habituate your horse to electric clippers, you get a helper to turn on the clipper at some distance from the horse while you give it some signals, such as to take one step forward, to stop, and to take on step backwards (see **Basic training,** below). In this way you encourage the horse to show a correct response (stepping forwards or backwards) instead of an unwanted response (avoidance behaviour). Partly because of overshadowing and partly because of reinforcing the correct behaviour, the horse will notice the sound of the clippers less and be more likely to notice your signals. In addition, if you reinforce its good behaviour by using positive reinforcement (stroking it on the withers or praising it), the training becomes a positive event for the horse.

Basic training: Training from the ground

Subjects: Teaching the horse to go forward
                Teaching the horse to stop
                'Parking' the horse
                Teaching the horse to yield
                Teaching the horse to go backwards
                Teaching the horse to lower its head

Teaching the horse to go forward:

◊   Pull forward on the lead rope.

◊   As soon as the horse takes a step forward, release the pressure.

◊   If the horse does not go forward, increase the pulling.

◊   If the horse still does not go forward, tap it repeatedly with the whip on its shoulder.

◊   As soon as the horse goes forward, stop the whip tapping and release the pressure on the lead rope.

Teaching the horse to stop:

◊   Pull backwards on the lead rope.

> **Remember:**
> **The first light pull is the signal to the horse to stop. The second stronger pull is unpleasant for the horse which means that it reacts to avoid the discomfort. The release of the pressure is the reinforcement that shows the horse that it has reacted correctly.**

◊   As soon as the horse stops, release the pressure.

◊   If the horse does not stop, pull more intensely, possibly several times.

◊   If the horse does not stop completely, repeat the pull backwards.

◊   As soon as it stops, release the pressure.

'Parking' the horse:

Once in a while you should let the horse stand still for some time, so that it learns to wait until it gets the signal to go forward. The horse is not allowed to decide when it may go.

◊   Once in a while, let the horse stand still for some time.

◊   Sometimes while it is standing, go around to the other side of the horse.

◊   If the horse goes forward, stop it and make it step back. Remember to release the pressure.

◊   If the horse steps back, give it the signal to go forward and stop it.

◊   If the horse goes to the side, make it yield back to where it was.

Continue to correct the behaviour of the horse until it stands still by itself for some time.

Stopping the horse and making it go forward:

There are different ways to make a horse go forward or stop. One way is to signal with a slight pull forwards or backwards with the lead rope or the reins. First you give the signal (pull forward or backward) before you yourself step forward or stop. In other words, you should not go forward or stop until the horse has reacted to the signal.

If you want to teach the horse to go forward or to stop when you yourself go forward or stop, you must start by doing so and then give the signal with the lead rope or reins. If you start the action before giving the signal the horse will learn to respond to your behaviour rather than to your signal (see **Learning through association,** page 66).

The best way to train a horse is to teach it to go forward on the signal from the lead rope because you will be able to intensify the signal, if necessary. If for instance you want the horse to go up into a trailer, it may not be enough if you go into the trailer. In that situation you need a signal that you can intensify, either by a stronger pull on the lead rope or by tapping with the whip.

To train the horse to go forward and to stop are the most important exercises. You need those reactions to teach the horse to go over things, through door openings, to go into a trailer, among other things. When you train these different situations, give the horse plenty of time to investigate whatever it is exposed to. Be patient. You should not fight with the horse but only use pressure from the lead rope and, if necessary, whip tapping to make it go forward.

Teaching the horse to yield:

◊   Stop the horse.

◊   Touch it with the whip on different places on its body to be sure that it is not afraid of the whip.

◊   Tap it with the whip on the lower part of the thigh until it moves its leg to the side.

◊   To make the horse step to the side by moving one leg over in front of the other leg, make sure that the horse is standing such that one leg is slightly in front of the other.

◊   When the horse has learned to yield for the whip tapping, teach it to yield to the pressure of your hand on its thigh.

Remember to teach the horse to yield to both sides.

Teaching the horse to go backwards:

◊   Stop the horse.

◊   Pull backwards on the lead rope.

◊   Release the pressure as soon as it takes one step backwards.

◊   If the horse does not react, press your thumb into its chest while you still pull backwards on the lead rope.

◊   Release both pressures as soon as the horse steps back.

Teaching the horse to lower its head:

Some trainers claim that lowering the head on a horse has a calming effect on the horse. Nobody knows, however, if that is true. Possibly, it only has an overshadowing effect on the horse (see **Overshadowing**, page 62). Whether it works one way or the other, it is a good idea to teach a horse to lower its head on command.

◊   Stop the horse.

◊   Pull down on the lead rope or reins.

◊   Release the pressure as soon as it lowers its head a little.

◊   Repeat the pull downwards until its head is all the way down.

◊   If the horse does not react pull alternatively on the two reins.

◊   Release the pressure as soon as the horse lowers its head.

BASIC TRAINING: TRAINING IN THE SADDLE

Subjects: Teaching the horse to go forward
                 Teaching the horse to stop
                 'Parking' the horse
                 Teaching the horse to yield
                 Teaching the horse to go backwards

Teaching the horse to go forward:

◊   Press with both legs.

◊   As soon as the horse goes one step forward, release the pressure.

◊   If the horse does not go forward press harder with the legs or, better yet, press repeatedly (like vibrating your legs).

◊   If the horse still does not go forward, tap it repeatedly with the whip on its shoulder (the same place you used when you trained from the ground), or on its side right behind your leg.

◊   As soon as the horse reacts by going forward, release the pressure from legs and whip.

Teaching the horse to stop:

◊   Put light tension on both reins.

◊   If the horse does not stop or does not slow down enough, repeat the tension.

◊   If the horse does not stop increase the tension until it stops.

◊   As soon as the horse stops, release the pressure.

For safety reasons it is important that all riding horses learn to stop from the pressure of the bit on the tongue and the lower jaw or, if using a bitless bridle, the pressure on the nose. Teaching a horse this reaction is similar to putting brakes on the horse. If it should get frightened by something and charge or if it is playful (for instance because it finally gets out of its stable) and also runs off uncontrolled, the only way to stop it is by pulling with sufficient force on the reins. But once the horse has learned this basic stop reaction it must also learn to stop or slow down in a more harmonious way. Usually riding instructors call it stopping the horse with the seat. In reality, the signal to the horse is given by several parts of the rider's body (a light tension with the legs, tightening of the abdominal and lower back muscles, and a light tension with the hands on the reins). Performed in this way the horse is more likely to stay in balance and be ready for the next exercise.

'Parking' the horse:

◊   A horse must be able to stand still on command, also when it has a rider on its back. This means that when you have stopped your horse it should stand still until you give it the signal to go forward again. It is not allowed to take the initiative to walk away when it thinks that it has been standing still long enough.

◊   But to stand still on command for a longer period is something the horse has to learn. It is not necessarily an innate characteristic.

◊   When you train your horse to stop, let it stand still once in a while for some time. Do not let it stand for too long a time in the beginning, and do not do it every time you stop.

◊   If the horse moves without being asked to do so, correct its behaviour at once. Let it go backwards if it has stepped forwards. Let it yield if it has stepped to the side. Be very consistent in your requirement to stand still.

Teaching the horse to yield:

◊   Stop the horse.

◊   Place right or left leg slightly further back on the side of the horse and press.

◊   When the horse takes a step to the side, release the pressure.

◊   If the horse does not respond, tap it with the whip on its thigh until it yields.

◊   As soon as it takes a step to the side, release the pressure of both leg and whip.

◊   When the horse has learned to yield, train the same in walk.

Teaching the horse to go backwards:

◊   Stop the horse.

◊   Ease your seat slightly more onto your thighs

◊   With your legs lightly against the horse's sides slightly behind the girth, give a brief signal to walk on with the legs

◊   Resist slightly with the hands by putting slight tension on the reins.

◊   Release the pressure as soon as the horse takes one step backwards.

◊   If you want the horse to take several steps backwards repeat the rein tension but release the pressure every time it takes a step.

Equitation Safety

When your horse can do these four exercises correctly (which means that it reacts when you give a signal using light pressure), you have all four legs of the horse under control.

To have control over its legs in all situations means that you are the one who decides. In that way you have the best chance to work with your horse harmoniously, and the risk of having an accident is smaller.

APPLIED TRAINING

◊   Of course, you cannot habituate your horse to all the different situations that can frighten it. If, for instance, you habituate it to the things mentioned here, it may still happen that it is frightened by something it has never seen before.

◊   But for one thing, a horse that has been habituated to plastic, to barking dogs, to motor cycle noise, etc. may react less intensely first time it sees an umbrella being opened. The more different things a horse has been exposed to, the less it will usually react when it meets something unknown. Although horses are not too good at generalizing (see **Generalization,** page 62), they can learn to remain reasonably calm when something new and unknown happens.

◊   For another, you will learn how your horse reacts when it gets frightened. For instance, you may learn that, even though it gets frightened, it does not turn around and run off but only jumps a small step to the side. And this knowledge means that it is also easier for you to remain calm in a touchy situation, so that your calmness can show the horse that there is nothing to be afraid of.

◊   Apart from training the situations described here, it is important to think about the situations you yourself meet on your ride, and to rank them according to how often they occur and how dangerous they are.

◊   If you on your ride come close to a busy road, you must habituate your horse to traffic. Part of the habituation happens if the horse is left on a pasture near a road. Another way is to ride near the road together with an experienced (and calm) horse.

◊   If you live in the countryside the probability of meeting tractors with various machines or harvesters is great.

◊   If your horse is stabled at a place where dogs are allowed to run free, you must habituate your horse to running dogs.

A prerequisite for the habituation to the different situations is that your horse has learned to react correctly to your signals, as described in the section Basic training. In other words, it must go forward on a light tug of the lead rope if you lead it, or from light pressure with your legs if you ride it, it must be able to stop on a light tension on lead rope or reins, and it must be able to 'park'. If, for instance, you want your horse to go over a piece of plastic lying on the ground, you exert a pressure forward. As soon as the horse takes a step forward you release the pressure. If the horse yields to the side, you turn it back with your hand (when leading) or leg (when riding), as described earlier.

HABITUATION IN GENERAL:

In principle, it does not matter whether you need to habituate your horse to the sound of a spray can or to the sound of a motor saw. The procedure is the same.

◊   The most important starting point is not to cause an accident in connection with the habituation of your horse. This means that you must not expose your horse to the stimulation in such a way that it becomes terrified. You must only expose it to the stimulation to the extent that it remains reasonably calm, so that you still have it under control.

◊   You must conduct the habituation in such a way that you do not have an accident if the unforeseen should happen and your horse panics. That means that also in this situation you must not be tied to your horse in any way. At all times you must be able to let go of it and be free of it. If you lead the horse on a lunge line, make sure you carry the line rolled up in your hand so that you do not accidentally get caught in it. And if the horse should get loose, it must not be able to run away. In other words, the training must be done in an enclosed area (a fenced-in riding arena, a paddock).

◊   If you lead your horse during the initial habituation, be careful not to stand in the way of the horse, if it should charge or jump. Do not stand right in front of it, if it should jump forward. When leading it past a scary object, walk on the same side as the object, so that it jumps away from you.

◊   Before you start the habituation you need to identify what exactly frightens your horse, or what exactly it is that you want your horse to get used to. Is it the sound (for instance from motor cycles), the smell (for instance of pigs), is it the sight (for instance of dogs running around) or is it the place it happens? If, for instance, your horse is afraid of motor cycles, maybe you can use the sound from a tape recording of the motor noise to habituate the horse. But if it is the movement of the bike, the colour, or the smell of it, you can only habituate the horse if you get a helper to drive around on a motor cycle. The sound of it would not be enough.

◊   When you have identified the source of your horse's fear you need to expose it to the thing, but at a reduced intensity, so that it does not become too frightened. If you use a tape recording for the exposure, turn down the volume. If it is the sight, the smell, or the movement, keep the horse so far from the object that it does not get scared. Reward the horse when it shows correct behaviour (that is, when it remains calm).

◊   Give the horse the signal to go one step forward and one back (see **Basic training,** page 68), while you expose it to a low intensity stimulation. (See also **Overshadowing,** page 62). Repeat the training but do not train for too long at a time. Wait a while (possibly till next day) and train again.

◊ Every time you train you stimulate the horse more and more. You gradually increase the volume, or you gradually reduce the distance. Do not proceed too fast but make sure that the horse remains reasonably calm. The calmer it is during the habituation the better. Remember to reward it for showing correct (that is calm) behaviour.

◊ In principle, the habituation can be done whether you stand beside the horse or you sit on its back. If you are afraid that the horse would suddenly react violently, do not sit on it. If you do the habituation from the ground, however, you need to repeat the training later on with you on its back. After all, it is while you are riding your horse that you want it to be calm.

◊ When you train with your horse, be careful not to over train. You should not train for too long a time, at the very most for 15–20 minutes. Your horse cannot concentrate on the training for more than that. You should rather wait till the next day (or wait several days) and start from the beginning. What the horse learned earlier it will still remember, so you can use its memory as kind of a 'warm up' period.

◊ In many cases you can make the habituation of an inexperienced horse easier if you let it follow an experienced horse.

Training your horse to stand still next to a mounting block:

In principle, the training is exactly the same as the training for 'parking' your horse, except that it happens next to a stool or mounting block. If the horse takes a step forward, make it go back. If it steps back, make it go forward. If it turns to the side, make it yield back.

Since you need the stool or mounting block to get up on the horse, this also has to be trained. Get up and down the stool or block a couple of times. When the horse stands still, sit up on the horse.

Training your horse to go away from the stable:

If your horse is afraid of going away from the stable, finish the daily ride 10 minutes earlier than usual. Walk down the road away from the stable for five minutes and five minutes back again. Next time you try it, ride down the road for eight minutes, then 10 minutes etc. Every time you ride you make the trip longer and longer, until the horse (and you) feels confident.

Training your horse to be separated from other horses during the ride:

Although it is always safest not to ride out alone, you may end up in a situation where you have to ride away from other horses, for instance if you have to go and get help. And even though a horse does not mind being ridden out alone, riding out together with other horses and then go away from them is a completely different situation. For that reason, it is a good idea to teach your horse to leave other horses during the ride. Use the same procedure as when you train it to go away from the stable. During the ride you ride a short distance away from the other horses, turn around, and ride back. If your horse gets very tense, do not ride further away than it is still able to see the other horses. Later, you can start riding behind a bush or something similar, so that visual contact is broken. When the horse has become used to this, you can start increasing the distance and the time the horses are separated.

Training your horse to go over things:

Horses do not like to go over bridges and other things that are not 'ground'. To have solid ground under its feet is extremely important for a flight animal. (That is probably why horses charge through water or mud – simply to get it over with as fast as possible).

◊   Teach your horse to go forward (see **Teaching the horse to go forward,** pages 68 and 71). Lead your horse up to the object. If necessary, use the whip to tap it forward. (see **Whip,** page 57). Give the horse time to check out the object. Be patient. Stop the horse when it has one or both front feet on the object. Make it stand still and maybe go back. In that way the process is not as hectic and it is easier to habituate the horse to go up and down the object. Thereafter, make the horse go forward till it is standing with all four feet on the object. Wait a few seconds before leading it on and down from the object. Repeat the exercise and also let the horse go backwards down from the object.

Habituating your horse to tractors:

> **Remember:**
> **When you habituate your horse to something that might scare it, it is always a good idea first to train from the ground before you train from the saddle.**

An easy way to habituate a horse to tractors is to lead or ride it out on a field that is being harvested. (Remember to get permission from the owner to do this.) Start walking at some distance from the tractor and work your way closer and closer to the tractor. Pay attention to the way your horse reacts and avoid letting it get too tense. When you can get close to the tractor, start following it around. A horse is less likely to get scared of objects that move away from it. Later, however, you also need to have the tractor approach the horse.

Next step in the habituation is to repeat it all when you ride by the tractor.

Habituating your horse to motor cycles:

In principle, the procedure is the same as with tractors, except that a motor cycle moves faster and may be noisier. Start the habituation by having the bike standing still and let the horse approach. After the initial 'checking out' the machine, let the driver rev up the engine. Later, let the motor cycle drive around, possibly also on a road to simulate a motor cycle driving by the horse.

Training your horse to pull things behind it:

Although you do not need to teach your horse to pull a cart, it is a good idea to habituate it to something that is dragging along behind it.

◊   If a branch gets stuck in its tail during a ride through the woods, it will be less likely to run off if it has been through this training.

◊   If some object is dragged over the ground near the horse (for instance a water hose), it will be less likely to get scared.

◊   In the winter it is tempting to pull your children's sledge or a skier with your horse. But before doing so, it is absolutely important first to habituate it to pulling things behind it.

When you train these situations, especially if you train from the saddle, it is extremely important that you hold on to the rope that you use for the pulling, in such a way that you can let go at any time if the horse should suddenly become afraid.

You must under no circumstance tie rope and object to the horse

Start by having a helper pull the object around, first at some distance and in front of the horse. An object that is moving away from a horse is usually less scary. Thereafter, let the horse walk next to the object, closer and closer to the object. And finally, let the object gradually move its way in behind the horse, as it is walking along.

Habituating your horse to plastic:

Something that can really frighten a horse is plastic (well, except for the plastic bag that carrots come in). Why it is so is difficult to say, but it may have something to do with the fact that plastic comes in many bright colours, it moves, it can make unusual sounds, and it probably smells unusual to horses. For that reason, it is almost impossible to habituate horses completely to plastic. Any habituation, however, may result in a less intense reaction, next time your horse meets plastic in a new and unknown situation.

Because of the many ways plastic is used, you have to decide which situation you want to focus on. Is it the plastic bag that somebody threw away on the side of the road? Is it the plastic tarpaulin the farmer puts over his firewood? Or is it the plastic strips hanging down in the doorway of the loose housing stable to keep out the wind?

The procedure is the same as with other scary things. Let the horse investigate the plastic. Be patient and give it enough time to check it out. Keep the plastic quiet in the beginning, but let it move later on (for instance, blow in the wind). Do it at some distance in the beginning if the horse is tense, and move gradually closer.

Remember, that just because the horse has become used to one kind of plastic in a certain place, does not necessarily mean that it will not get frightened by another kind of plastic, or the same kind but in another place.

Teach your horse to love plastic

If you want to teach your horse not to be afraid of plastic and at the same time impress your fellow riders, Janne Winther Christensen who is one of the leading horse research persons in Denmark, has described an effective way. Take a plastic bag, for instance a feed bag that smells good, and put it on the ground. When the horse approaches and sniffs the bag you praise it and give it a treat. If the horse takes hold of the bag and lifts it up, you praise it again and give it a treat. Repeat it several times but do not train more than five to ten minutes which equals 10–20 treats. Instead, wait till next day to train again. When the horse has connected the touch of the bag with a treat you stop giving it a treat when it just touches the bag. The horse will become frustrated and start to push the bag around, at which point you give it another treat. If the horse does not start to pick up the bag you can put a little bit of feed into it so that the horse starts to bite into it and to pick it up, which you also reward with a treat. When the behaviour of the horse has been established, you give it a command (for instance 'take the bag') while placing it on the ground. Later you should use different bags and possibly also a larger piece of plastic.

Finally, you should train in different locations, both when you stand next to the horse and when you are sitting on its back.

When the horse has learned it all, you only need to give it the command when you meet some plastic on your ride. The horse will then go up to the plastic, touch it, and expect a treat (which you should have along in your pocket).

Habituating your horse to dogs

When you ride out in nature, it may easily happen that you stir up some wildlife. Many horses get quite scared in that situation. Many horses get quite scared in that situation. Rabbits or pheasants that sit quite still and do not flee until you almost step on them can make a horse panic.

One way of reducing a horse's tendency to be frightened is to habituate it to dogs running around nearby. As you lead or ride your horse around in the arena, have somebody play ball or stick with one or several dogs. The more the horse gets used to dogs almost running between its legs (but only almost!), the more likely it is to stay reasonably calm when out in the woods.

STARTING A YOUNG HORSE

Horses are not born to carry a rider. Even though we have bred riding horses for thousands of years, the feeling of something heavy on the back still means danger. Domestic horses react exactly like wild horses when there is something on their back. They buck, jump to the side and they charge.

The process of starting a horse starts by training it from the ground, as described earlier (see **Basic training**, page 68). It is important that it learns to stop, to stand still, and to go forward on a signal. Do the training in an enclosed area (a riding arena). If the horse is tense being alone, have another horse present.

Apart from the ground training, you should also habituate the horse to having a bridle on and a bit in its mouth. The easiest way is to put on the bridle (without reins) and a soft bit (for instance a rubber bit) while the horse stands in its stable or in a small enclosure. Leave the bridle on for 10 minutes or more so that the horse can chew on the bit and get used to the feeling of it. If necessary, repeat the experience over several days.

Repeat the groundwork but this time with the bridle and reins. Use the reins to stop the horse and to get it to go forward.

Next, the horse needs to get used to having a girth around the chest, to having a saddle cloth or numnah on its back, and later a saddle, before you start the actual breaking in. If the horse has learned to be lunged, it is a good idea to lunge it with the saddle on, both in walk and in trot, to give it the feeling of having the saddle on also when it moves. If the horse starts to buck, stop it immediately with the lunge line by making the circle smaller. You do not want saddle plus bucking to become a habit. In the beginning, let the stirrups lie across the saddle, so they do not slam into the sides of the horse. Later, however, you should let them hang down so that the horse gets used to having them bang against its sides.

The safest way to do the actual start in is that one person holds the horse with bridle and reins, and another person is the rider. The mounting of the horse can be done with or without a saddle. If the horse reacts violently during the start, it is actually easier to jump off the horse when it does not have a saddle on.

Stand next to the horse at the level of its chest. Place both hands on its back and jump up and down as if you would jump up on it. If it tries to avoid you, stop it immediately, and do the jumping a little less intensely. Repeat until the horse does not try to get away. Put more and more weight on its back and jump up and lean over its back. Do every step gradually and be sure that the horse stays reasonably calm. If it tries to avoid you, stop it immediately and repeat the jumping etc.

When the horse is sufficiently calm, jump up and lay across its back on your stomach. If necessary, have your helper help you up. While you lay there, let the horse go forward a few steps. If it should try to run away, you can easily push away from the horse. Repeat until it remains calm.

While you lie on its back, touch it with hands and arms both on its right side and on its rump. Let it walk around a little while you are hanging on it. When it is quite calm you can slowly bring your right leg up on its rump and, if it is still calm, bring it down on its right side. Do not sit up right away but lean forward over its neck. Walk around a bit and wait to sit up straight till the horse is calm.

When the horse has got used to you sitting up straight, both when it is standing still and when it is walking, it is time to teach it the signals to go forward and to stop, when the signals come from the rider. To make sure that the horse does not run off, it is a good idea that the helper has a lunge line attached to the bit, so that you can use the reins. Press lightly with your legs. If the horse does not react, get the helper to pull the horse forward at the same time that you press with your legs. Repeat the pressure with your legs and, if nothing happens, then pull forward. Usually, the horse learns after a few trials the meaning of the leg pressure. Remember only to press lightly and to release the pressure as soon as it moves forward.

Although the horse is now started, you are still a long way away from the point when you can ride it under different conditions, such as alone in the indoor arena, together with other horses, outdoors, etc. Progress slowly and avoid exposing the horse to situations that make it react violently.

Chapter 5

Safety related advice

FIRST AID

Falling from a horse

◊   Some riders claim that you have to fall off a horse 100 times before you can call yourself an experienced rider. This is nonsense and an old-fashioned attitude towards horse riding. To ride in a safe way you should do everything to avoid falling off a horse. Another matter is that, when you are an active rider it is almost impossible completely to avoid falling off your horse.

◊   Another old-fashioned attitude is that, when a rider has fallen off her horse, she must immediately get back up on the horse, to avoid developing a fear of riding. Also this rule is nonsense. If a rider has been seriously injured, possibly in a way that is not evident (such as concussion or internal bleeding), the worst place to be is on the back of a horse.

Injuries to the back

◊   When a rider falls off a horse, the most serious risk is that she suffers an injury to the spine, either in the neck region or in the lumbar area. Neither a riding helmet nor a safety vest can protect these areas, should a worst case scenario happen.

◊   If you suspect that a rider has suffered an injury of this kind, it is of utmost importance NOT to move the person. If the rider has broken her back, any movement of the break can result in a serious exacerbation of the injury.

At the slightest suspicion that a rider has broken her back, she must only be moved if there is an immediate danger for her safety in remaining on the spot. Otherwise, only emergency personnel may move the patient (physician, ambulance driver)

The rider in the picture has fallen off his horse and has called the emergency service on his mobile phone.

When the emergency personnel have arrived the rider is carefully moved to a stiff board so that the spine can be stabilised. Not until x-rays have been taken of the spine to make sure that nothing is broken, can the patient be moved to a softer mattress.

Luckily the rider in the picture had 'only' broken an ankle.

Concussion

Even when a rider wears a riding helmet, a fall from the horse can cause a concussion. The symptoms of a concussion (nausea, dizziness, and headache) may not become obvious until after some time. For that reason it is important to let a rider who has received a severe blow to the head, sit quietly for 10–20 minutes before getting back up on the horse.

When a rider falls off a horse it is important, first, to help the rider. Not until the state of the rider is under control (and for instance an ambulance has been called), is it time to take care of the horse, if somebody else has not already done so. Apart from catching it, it also needs to be checked for injuries and, if necessary, treated.

Kick from a horse

◊   When a rider has been kicked by a horse she will obviously feel severe pain. Apart from the pain it is, however, important to be aware of the fact that the person can have internal injuries that are not visible. A kick on the chest can break ribs that can then puncture a lung. A kick to the lower body can cause internal bleeding that does not show up until after some time.

◊   At the slightest suspicion of this kind of injury, it is absolutely vital that the rider gets proper medical attention.

> **It is better to bring an injured rider to the Accident and Emergency department and find out that nothing serious has happened than not to bring a rider to A & E and later find out that something serious has happened**

First aid courses

A couple of good pieces of advice:

◊   Every rider should take a first aid course. Every riding stable and riding school should arrange first aid courses regularly. Some day your own safety might also depend on this arrangement.

◊   Tetanus bacteria thrive in horse manure. Make sure that you have a valid tetanus vaccination.

◊   If you wear glasses and cannot see much without them, maybe you should have an extra pair nearby and, for instance, bring them along when you go cross country.

IN CASE OF FIRE

In case of fire in a stable it is important to prioritize your actions, which means to do the important things first.

1. Call the fire brigade.
2. Call for help to get the horses out.
3. Get the horses out.

4. Try to extinguish the fire as much as you can.

> **It is extremely important to call for help both to extinguish the fire and to get the horses out BEFORE you jump into action yourself.**

1. Call the fire brigade first:

   Remember to give an exact address,
   how big the fire is,
   and that there are horses in the stable

> **Remember: It is better that the fire brigade comes out, even though it later turns out to be unnecessary, than if the fire brigade does not come out and it later turns out that it actually was necessary.**

2. Before you start letting out the horses you should call somebody to help you. Call the neighbours or stop a car driving by and ask them to call for help.

3. Depending on how big the fire is, especially depending on how much smoke it makes, the best course of action is to lead each horse by itself. To open all stable doors and expect the horses to run out on their own is too optimistic. Most often they remain in their stable. Usually, that is the place where they feel safest.

   You also have to get the horses out to a pasture or paddock, at least far enough away so that they do not run back into the stable. Because many horses feel safest in their home stable, they are very likely to run back, despite smoke and fire.

4. Not until all horses are safe can you start extinguishing the fire. But remember not to put yourself in a dangerous situation. Let the professional fire people do that.

Hopefully, you will never need these advices.
   But the following pieces of advice are important:

◊ In every stable there should be fire extinguishers, fire blankets, a stretcher, and a first aid kit.

Everybody who visits the stable regularly should know where these objects are kept.

◊ It is a good idea that the person responsible for the stable from time to time holds a meeting where it is discussed what to do in case of fire. Where should the horses be taken, from whom can you get help, etc. An even better idea is to hold fire exercises and practice taking out all horses, finding the fire extinguishing equipment, etc.

◊ Finally, it is important that electrical installations, wires, electric outlets and other things are checked regularly, preferably by an authorized person.

Chapter 6

Buying a horse from a safety point of view

IT is often a somewhat risky business to buy a horse. Apart from the health aspects, there may be questions about how well trained it is and about its behaviour in general. Is it easy to handle? Can it go together with other horses, and many other questions.

A topic that, unfortunately, is low on the list of things to consider is the safety aspect. Does it turn its hind end towards you when you approach or does it lay back its ears? Does it stand still when you put on a halter, does it walk quietly beside you when you lead it? Is it safe in traffic? Does it go into a trailer? Is it afraid of baby buggies? Preferably, you should make a list of all the safety aspects that are important for you, before going to look at the horse, so that you do not forget something 'in the heat of the discussion'.

As far as safety is concerned it is important to think about what you want to use your horse for. Not what your future plans eventually are, but how you want to ride it now. Are you going to use it for leisure riding, for riding competitions, is it going to be housed in an individual stable or be out in pasture most of the time together with other horses?

When you have worked your way through these and similar questions you need to make sure that the horse you are looking at will live up to your expectations. Remember that it is not enough to ask the seller. His or her answers will undoubtedly be positive. You need to have things demonstrated. Are you (or better yet, the seller) able to ride away from the stable and away from other horses? Is it as easy to load the horse into a trailer as the seller claims? And do not accept bad excuses for not having it demonstrated ('our trailer has a puncture!'). If your horse is going to be kept in group housing or if it is supposed to be able to go in pasture together with other horses, you need to find out how social it is. Is it used to being with other horses or has it always been kept in individual housing? Even the best-trained and obedient but poorly socialized horse is not worth much, if it is stabled in a place where all horses are turned out in pasture daily.

If the horse you are interested in has some safety-related faults, you have to consider what it means to you. Is it a behaviour problem that you yourself can correct or do you need professional help? If so, remember that that can be a costly and long lasting undertaking.

If you consider buying a green horse (that is, a horse that has not been ridden before), you have to think about how the training should be done. Are you yourself experienced and good enough to do it, or are you dependent upon professional help? If so, do you know who can do it and how much it will cost you? Remember that a three-month period with a professional rider may not be the best way to get an obedient and safe horse. Maybe the horse you are thinking of needs more time to learn the many things a horse must learn to be obedient and safe.

It is important that you define as clearly as possible what you expect of the horse, that you check out its talents and, if something is missing, that you think about what you can do to rectify them.

To parents of children who want a horse

If your child has a burning desire to ride a horse or a pony, obviously it is your duty to ensure that it is done in a safe way. To work with a horse or a pony can be a valuable activity for a child. To be responsible for a living being, to care for it, and to make sure that its needs are fulfilled is a healthy way to teach the child responsibility. As statistics show, however, this healthy activity can also be dangerous. In some countries up to ninety percent of all horse-related accidents happen to girls at the ages 12 to 16 years. (Most boys in the same age groups are not riding horses. They play ball, and the accidents they have are much less serious).

Before you allow your child to ride at a riding school you must ensure that the people running the school are aware of safety and that they teach riders about safety. Unfortunately, this is not always the case. If you do not consider yourself qualified for such an evaluation, you should get somebody to do it who knows about horses and horse riding. Incidentally, you do not have to be a specialist in the subject to evaluate a riding school. You just have to notice how the place looks. Are the tools and the equipment put away or left all over the place? What impression do the horses make? Are they calm and well behaved? What about the riding teacher and the stable personnel? Are they calm and patient towards horses and riders? What does a riding lesson look like? Are the horses going around in a line, one after the other, or are they running around in the riding arena in an uncontrolled way?

If you plan to buy your child a horse or a pony, wait to do so until the child has been riding for quite some time. For one thing, it is very important that your child has a basic knowledge about how to ride and handle a horse in a safe way. For another, you must make sure that horses and riding really is the thing for your child. A horse is a living being that demands attention all year round, including when it rains and is cold. A horse is not a piece of gymnastic equipment that you can store in a cupboard until spring. And when you have bought a horse or a pony it can be very difficult to sell it again, either because it may be hard to find a buyer, or because you or your child have become emotionally attached to it. Besides, it is not nice for the horse to be moved to a new place yet again.

When you have bought a horse or a pony for your child your duty as a responsible parent has not stopped. You still have to make sure that the horse is stabled in a responsible way, that it is well taken care of, and that what your child does with the horse is done in a safe and responsible way. If for some reason you are not able to check these things regularly, you have to ensure that a sufficiently competent person is doing it for you, for instance the person responsible for the stable.

Speaking of children: do not let smaller children be near horses without supervision, no matter if the horses are free in pasture or tied up somewhere. For one thing, a horse may take a step to the side (to reach some grass or something similar) and accidentally hit or step on the child. For another, a horse may attack a small child, possibly because it considers the child a threat (see **Social groups,** page 40).

Part 2: Applied information

The section describes 70 different conditions or situations that are known to be potentially risky and that can hurt you. The situations are categorized under the following headings:

Horses in pasture
Horses in the stable
Riding
Riding in the riding arena
Riding cross country
Riding problem horses
Trailer transport of horses

In each situation is described

1. why the situation may be risky
2. what you can do to minimize the risk
3. what you should do or not do if a dangerous situation happens

> **Important things are mentioned in a box like this.**

Specially important things, for instance things that can be dangerous and things you absolutely should know are placed next to a warning sign.

Chapter 7

Horses in the pasture

Approaching a horse

1. What is the risk?

> When you approach a horse that is free in pasture or in a paddock there is always the risk that you can get kicked or bitten by the horse. The risk is greater if several horses go together.
>
> If you approach a horse that is not aware of you, it can become surprised and kick out in your direction as it is running away.
>
> If the horse does not want to get caught, it may try to chase you away by biting or kicking you.
>
> If the horse is playful it may try to play with you by running around and kicking out after you. The risk is greater if you try to catch the horse by running after it.

If you bring a treat for the horse when you go to fetch it from the pasture, the other horses may approach you and they may start fighting with each other.

It is always dangerous to be near horses that fight

2. How can you avoid the risk?

When you approach the horse, you must let it know that you are coming, for instance by calling out its name. You need to approach it calmly. You must not run.

When you approach the horse, do it from the side, preferably the left side, and a little to the front. Then it is easier for the horse to see you.

If the horse has a tendency to run away, for instance towards other horses or away from the stable, you should try to approach it from the direction in which it is most likely to run. In that way you may cut off its flight opportunity and there is a greater chance that it will stand still.

If your horse knows that you have a treat with you, undoubtedly it will be easier to get hold of it. You should, however, only feed your own horse to avoid the other horses coming over to you.

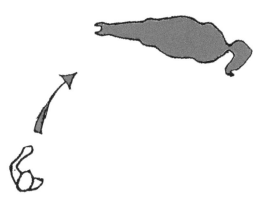

3. What should you do if the horse kicks out after you or tries to bite you or if it continues to move away from you?

    Keep out of its reach. Stand still and wait till it calms down.

    Continue to approach the horse quietly. In most cases, it will realize that it cannot get rid of you at which point it will let you approach it.

    If it is still aggressive, you need to get help to catch it. In addition, you need to try to find out why it does not like to be caught. Is it not socialized enough (see **Socialization,** page 40)? Is it housed next to one of its enemies? Is it ridden too harshly? There can be many reasons why a horse does not want to leave its pasture.

Catching a horse

1. What is the risk?

    If the horse runs away it is tempting to run after it. The horse may think that it is being chased or that you are playing with it. In both cases it may kick out after you.

    It is also tempting to try to punish it if it is running by you, for instance by hitting it with the lead rope. That is also a bad idea because that can also make it kick out. Besides, it will make it harder to catch the horse next time. Horses learn (in a split second!) that they can get rid of you by running away.

2. How can you avoid the risk?

    Start by going calmly after the horse without chasing it. After a while it may realize that it cannot get rid of you. For some horses it may take a while before they realize it but it is usually worth the investment of the effort. Next time you want to catch it, it will not be quite as difficult.

    The best thing to do is to get help from a couple of people. But also when you are several people to catch the horse you need to do it in a calm and quiet way. Try to get the horse into a corner. Most horses will then give up and let you approach.

When a horse feels surrounded, it is more likely to kick out. Therefore, you need to be extra careful in that situation and extra calm.

3. What can you do if the horse absolutely refuses to get caught?

Try to entice the horse to come home by bringing home the other horses in the pasture.

Get the horse to come over to the gate by taking the other horses out of the paddock. (Remember that this is only possible if the horse respects the fencing and stays in the paddock when alone.)

Make a small enclosure, for instance in front of the gate, and entice the horse in with some food. Usually it is easier to approach a horse when it knows that it cannot escape in the small area.

To make it easier to catch the horse in the future you must train it to come to you or, at least, not to run away from you. Start the training in a small enclosure (such as its stable), later in the indoor arena or a fenced in riding arena, later in the paddock when no other horses are around. If the horse refuses to stand still in these situations it can be necessary to put a long rope or lunge line on the horse so that you can hold it when you approach.

You should also try to find out why the horse does not want to get caught. Is it because it does not want to come to the stable to get a saddle on, for instance because of back problems? Is it your riding or training method that it does not like? Does it not like to be stabled because of one of the neighbouring horses? Do other people have a problem catching the horse, or is it only you that have those problems?

Leading a horse home from the pasture

1. What is the risk?

If the horse does not want to go home it may turn away from you, free itself, and run back to where it was. Besides this being irritating, you can get hurt if you try to hold back the horse.

When you lead a horse with one hand and you need to open a gate with the other hand, plus possibly chase other horses away that are not supposed to get out, it is easy to have an accident. Your horse may try to push its way through the gate, either to get home or to get away from the other horses. The other horses may try to push their way through the gate. The horses may start fighting because they are too close together.

If you need to open an electric fence, either you or your horse may accidentally touch the fence and receive a shock. Horses can react violently if they get an electric shock.

If the electric wire is lying on the ground the horse can get it wrapped around a leg which is dangerous whether the wire is electric or not.

If several horses are brought home from a pasture that is relatively close to the stable, it is tempting to let them run home by themselves, possibly all the way into the stable and into their respective stables. If the horses are eager to get home (for instance if there is feed waiting in their troughs), they may slide out and fall if they are going around a corner, and it may get crowded in front of the door into the stable. Besides, the distribution of horses in the stables may not result in the right horse ending up in the right stable. The risk that both horses and people get hurt in the following chaos is great.

2. What should you do to avoid an accident?

In a split second before the horse turns around to run away from you when you lead it, it starts by turning its head (see **Intention movements,** page 41). If you know that the horse has a history of running off, you can turn its head slightly towards you while you lead it home. In that way it is easier for you to control the horse because it is less likely to turn away and run off.

If the other horses in the pasture try to push their way through the gate, you may first try to chase them as far away as possible so that they are not in the way. The safest way to do so is to get somebody to help you.

When you reach the gate, give your horse a signal to stop in front of the gate before you start to open it (see **Stopping a horse and making it go forward,** page 70). Then you open the gate, give the horse a signal to go forward (see **Stopping a horse and making it go forward,** page 70), turn it around and stop it, at which point you close the gate. Finally, you give the horse a signal to turn around again and to go away from the gate.

> **Remember to give your horse a signal to stop and a signal to go forward!**
> **Every time.**
> **You are the one who decides what your horse should do.**

If you bring in the horses in a group and let them run in by themselves, it is a good idea to have a collection area in front of the stable from where you can lead in each horse individually into its own stable. In that way you avoid the chaos in the aisle way of the stable or in the yard in front of the stables, and the horses have a chance to calm down before they get into the stable.

(See also **Leading a horse,** page 102.)

3. What should you do if something goes wrong?

If the other horses in the pasture manage to get out, you can see what to do under **Catching horses that have escaped** (page 98).

If your horse has received an electric shock and is afraid of getting near the fence, try to calm it down and to lead it quietly forward towards the place. Give the horse plenty of time to 'investigate' the spot. If it still refuses, let it follow another horse that is not afraid of the place. (See also **Habituation in general,** page 75 and **Riding past scary things,** page 147.)

If the horses start fighting while you try to get out, keep an eye on which horses are involved in the fight and try to seek protection behind a horse that is not involved in the fight. As soon as you have a chance to get away safely, do so and go and get help to solve the problem.

If your horse is kept in a pasture together with other horses and you often have to get it home to the stable without the other horses following, you should train all the horses to be led individually from the field and back without disturbance from the remaining horses. The best way to do the training is if three or four people participate.

First, one person goes in and takes hold of a horse, takes it to the gate and leads it out of the pasture. The other people stay ready to chase the other horses away from the gate if it should be necessary.

After a short while the horse is led back into the pasture and again, the other horses are chased away from the gate, if necessary.

The whole procedure is repeated with the other horses, one at a time. Usually the herd calms down after a few repetitions so that one horse can be taken out or in without the other horses being involved.

Possibly, the whole procedure must be repeated a few times the following days until all horses have learned the procedure.

Leading a horse through a gate:

1. Lead the horse up to the gate.
2. Give it the signal to stop.
3. Open the gate.
4. Give the horse the signal to go forward.
5. Turn the horse around and give it the signal to stop.
6. Close the gate.
7. Give the horse the signal to go forward, turn it around, and go away from the gate.

A. When the opening of the gate is on the left side, it is easiest to lead the horse from its left side so that you can hold the horse with your right hand and open the gate with your left hand.

B. When the opening of the gate is on the right side, it is easiest to lead the horse from its right side so that you can hold the horse with your left hand and open the gate with your right hand.

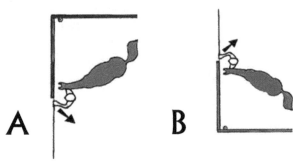

Leading a horse out to pasture:

1. What is the risk?

   If a horse is excited to get out, it can bolt and pull you along, it can run over you, or it can start by bucking and kicking out, possibly in your direction, as soon as it is let loose, and running away.

   If the horse is new and unknown to the horses already on the field, they may come over to 'greet' the newcomer, which easily can result in a fight.

   If several people lead their horses to pasture but do not let them loose simultaneously, the first loose horses may run off and incite the other horses that are not yet free to run off.

   > **To let a horse free on the way into the pasture is dangerous because it may start running and kicking out in your direction.**

2. What should you do to avoid an accident?

   You lead your horse up to the gate and give it the signal to stop.

   Then you open the gate and give your horse the signal to go forward.

   When you are through the gate you turn your horse around and stop it.

   When you have closed the gate again, you give the horse the signal to go forward. You go a short distance into the pasture so that you are free of the fence.

   Then you turn the horse around again so that it is standing in the direction from where you came and you stop it.

   Now you can loosen the lead rope but as you move away from the horse, keep an eye on it till you are out of its reach.

If the horse is a newcomer to the other horses, you need to have one or two helpers along who can keep the other horses away until you have let the new horse loose and got away from it.

   If there are several people bringing horses to the pasture, you need to synchronize when to let them loose so that it happens simultaneously.

3. How can you avoid an accident?

If the pasture is far away from the stable, it is tempting to sit on the horse and to ride it there (or to ride it home when you pick it up). But to ride bareback can be difficult if you are used to a saddle. You can easily lose your balance and to steer a horse with a halter and a lead rope is difficult unless the horse has learned to be ridden in this way.

And if it is all done in sandals or in bare feet without a riding helmet, a serious accident can happen, especially if the horse is excited about getting out (or home).

Catching horses that have escaped from their pasture:

1. What is the risk?

Horses that have escaped from their pasture always constitute a serious risk. They can get hurt but, what is worse, they constitute a big risk for other people depending upon where they go. Especially if they are on their way towards a busy road, it is important to take action immediately and effectively. But on a less busy road loose horses also constitute a risk.

2. How can you avoid an accident?

If the horses are near a busy road, it may be necessary to call the police. Only the police can stop the traffic in such a way that neither people nor horses are hurt. On a less busy road it may be possible to ask the driver of a car to stop and turn on the hazard warning lights so that other cars are sufficiently warned.

If several horses have escaped it is important to get help to catch them again. It is too risky to try to get them back alone.

How to proceed depends on how excited the horses are. If they are reasonably calm, try to get hold of one or a few horses. If you can lead them back into the pasture, the other horses will usually follow.

If the horses are very agitated or if they enjoy their freedom, they will probably run away when you approach. Therefore, approach them from the opposite side to their pasture or stable so that they run home when you approach them.

If there are sufficient people, walk (don't run) towards the group approximately 10 m between one another so that you form a kind of 'wall'. In that way you have a better chance of stopping them from running in the wrong direction.

> **Do not ever try to catch a horse by running after it.**
> **That will just make it run away from you faster.**

If at all possible, try to drive the horses into an enclosed area (a field, a yard or something similar). When the horses feel that they are 'fenced in', they are more likely to calm down and be easier to get hold of.

Remember to check the fencing of the pasture before the horses are turned back out. If they have escaped by going through the fence, they might try it again, unless it is repaired.

To halter or not to halter

   1.   What is the risk of having the horse wear a halter?

   ◊   People disagree on the question of whether a horse should always wear a halter or not when it is turned out in a pasture.

   ◊   People also disagree on the question of whether a horse should wear a halter when it is standing in its stable or kept in loose housing.

   ◊   The advantage of having a halter on a horse when it is on its own is that it is easier to get hold of and to handle once you have gotten hold of it.

   ◊   The disadvantage is that the horse could get the halter caught in something, for instance if it rubs against a fencepost with nails or old hinges or something like that. For horses wearing shoes on their hind legs, there is a risk that they get the shoe caught in the halter if the horse scratches itself in the neck with a hind leg (which they are actually able to do!). A horse that does not get help immediately if that happens, may die within a short time from exhaustion trying to get loose.

2. How can you avoid an accident?

◊ Without a doubt, it is safest always to have a halter on your horse when it is by itself. In that way, it is easier to get hold of and easier to handle, once you have gotten hold of it. This is true whether the horse is in the pasture, in a loose housing system, or standing alone in its stable. For one thing, the horse may escape. For another, you may need to get your horse out of the stable in a hurry, for instance in case of a fire.

◊ To prevent the halter of the horse getting caught in something, it is important that it fits the horse reasonably tightly around the neck (but loose around the muzzle so that the horse can still open its mouth). In addition, it is a good idea to use a halter that can break if the horse pulls on it with great force.

◊ In general, it is important to make sure that old nails, hinges, and other hardware are not situated in the walls where the horses are kept. Not only can they get their halters caught, but they can also get hurt in other ways. And so can you yourself. Regularly check stable, fence posts, and other surfaces and get the old stuff removed.

3. What should you do if an accident happens?

◊   A horse whose halter is caught in something will often react very violently to get loose. In that case, you need to approach it carefully and keep clear of those parts of its body that it uses to fight (legs, head and neck).

◊   If you are afraid that you cannot free the horse yourself, make sure you get somebody to help you.

◊   The fastest solution to the problem is to cut through the halter with a sharp knife. Be careful of the reaction of the horse when it gets loose. If it is pulling with great force at the moment you cut it loose, it may fall over backwards or something similar so stay clear of it.

◊   If you do not have a sharp knife handy, it can be necessary to put a rope around the neck of the horse and pull in the opposite direction until you can free the halter. Obviously, this is easier if several people can participate in the pulling.

Chapter 8

Horses in the stable

Going up to a horse:

    1.   What is the risk?

◊   When you go up to a horse, whether it is kept in a stable or in loose housing, it can be difficult to see if the horse has noticed you or not. It can actually be standing with its eyes open and still sleep or doze so that it does not notice what happens around it.

◊   Horses kept in stables that open out towards an aisle way or towards a yard can stand with their head out and sleep. If you touch such a horse as you walk by, it can become so surprised that it either jumps back or that it bites you in self-defence.

◊   If your horse is kept in loose housing, there is a risk that the other horses come up to you as you get your own horse. Some of the other horses may start fighting.

    2.   What should you do to avoid an accident?

◊   When you approach the horse, make sure that it notices that you are coming, for instance by talking to the horse.

◊   In the case of a horse standing with its head out of the stable, you should either go by without touching it or you need to warn it about your presence before touching it.

◊   If your horse is kept in loose housing, you need to take it out of the group before tying it up.

Leading a horse:

    1.   What is the risk?

◊ When you lead a horse it may not want to come along so that it turns away and runs off. If you only hold on to the halter alone, it may get loose just by turning its head away from you.

◊ If the horse walks behind you it may step on your heels and cause you to stumble. If it is frightened by something behind it, it may jump forward into you. But most importantly, you cannot keep an eye on the horse when it goes behind you..

◊ If you wear spurs (which is a bad idea, see **Spurs,** page 134), and the horse steps on one of them you can easily stumble.

◊ If you lead the horse from its left side and you need to turn left, your horse may take a 'short-cut' and step on your heels.

◊ If you lead the horse in a bridle, using the reins, your horse may step on the reins if you accidentally let them hang down. This can hurt the horse or damage the reins.

2. What should you do to avoid an accident?

◊ The safest way to lead a horse is to use a lead rope attached to the halter or reins on the bridle. You should hold rope or reins with your right hand about 10 cm from the head of the horse and the free end with your left hand. If the horse turns its head and neck to the side so that you lose your grip with your right hand, you can still hold the horse with your left. In other words, you get chance number two to hold the horse.

◊ If the horse turns its head away from you in order to run off, you must stop its movement as soon as it starts turning away (see **Intention movements,** page 41).

◊ When you lead the horse, you should be at the level of the middle of the horse's neck, and approximately an arm's length to the side of the horse. In that way it does not walk into you and you can keep an eye on what it is doing.

◊ Some riders learn that, to turn a horse they must walk around the horse to prevent that the horse stepping on them. If you lead from the horse's left side and you need to turn to the right, it makes sense to gradually walk in front of the horse while leading it to the right. If you need to turn to the left, however, the method does not work. Instead, you must get the horse to walk around you to the left. That means that you need to maintain your distance to the horse so that it does not make a 'short-cut' and step on you.

◊ When leading a horse in the bridle, some riders learn that the reins must stay over the neck of the horse to prevent them from falling down and getting stepped on. If you are only going a short distance, for instance from the stable into the indoor arena, it is a good idea. But if you need to lead it a longer distance, it is safer to take the reins down over the head of the horse and hold them as you hold a lead rope, that is, with your right hand approximately 10 cm from the bit and your left hand on the free end of the reins. If you hold the reins with just one hand, you must collect the loose end in that hand, too, so that it does not hang down.

◊ The 'correct' side to lead a horse is from the left side. It is a good idea, however, once in a while to train to lead from the right side. A horse should learn to be led from both sides. If for instance you need to lead two horses simultaneously, one of them must go on your left side.

> **But most importantly:**
> **Do not wrap lead rope or reins around your hand or arm. Only hold them so that you can let go of them if the horse should run off**

Tying up a horse:

1. What is the risk?

◊ A horse that is tied to a wall or a fence post can get scared and start pulling back. Some horses react strongly when they feel resistance from the halter which makes them pull even more. If the rope or halter should break, it can happen that the horse falls backwards.

Never go too close to a horse that is tied up if it starts pulling back

◊ Tying up a horse with a panic snap (a snap that opens up when the horse pulls strongly) or tying it with a piece of baling twine prevents the horse from pulling so hard that it falls. It does not, however, prevent it from pulling and from getting loose.

◊ If your horse pulls back while you are tying it, you may hurt your fingers if you have them 'inside the knot'.

2. How can you avoid an accident?

◊ A horse that is tied up with an elastic rope will not feel the resistance as strongly as when it is tied with a rope because it gives way to some extent. As a result, it is less likely to pull back.

◊ A horse that has the bad habit of pulling back can be tied between two vertical posts or it can be tied in the aisle way between two rows of stables. If it pulls back, the ropes offer less resistance so that the horse is less likely to pull back.

◊ The safest way to tie up a horse that is likely to pull back is to place it where it has a wall or a bar behind it, which makes it impossible for the horse to pull back.

◊ Be careful not to have your fingers 'in the knot' while you tie it.

◊   Teaching a horse to go forward by pulling forward on the lead rope (see **Training from the ground,** page 68) will make it less likely that it pulls back when tied.

3.   What should you do if a horse pulls back?

◊   When a tied horse starts pulling back, it can happen that rope or halter breaks so that the horse falls backwards. Therefore, you must never come too close to the horse.

◊   From a safe distance, you may try to chase the horse forward by waving a jacket or something similar behind it and by yelling at it to get its attention.

◊   As soon as it goes forward, go up to it from the side and calm down the horse.

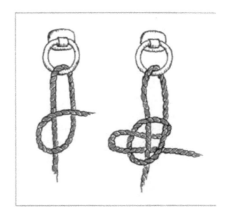

Safety knot. Tie the rope with a safety knot, that is, a knot that can easily be untied even if the horse has pulled it tight.

◊   Remember: You must only tie your horse to objects that can hold the horse if it should pull back.

You must only tie your horse to, for instance

◊   a solid ring in the wall

◊   a bar that is fastened to something

◊   a post standing solidly in the ground

◊   a horse trailer

You must not tie your horse to a wheelbarrow, garden furniture or similar 'loose' objects

◊   If several horses are tied next to each other, place them with enough distance between them so that they do not start fighting with each other and, for instance, kick each other.

◊   Do not tie up a horse in an area with loose horses. For one thing, the tied up horse cannot get away should it be necessary. For another, one of the loose horses may try to get in front of the tied up horse causing it to pull back.

Working around a horse:

1. What is the risk?

◊ When you are close to a horse there is always the danger that it gets frightened and tries to jump to the side or forward. If you stand between the horse and a wall, you can get crushed or stepped on.

◊ If the horse kicks, the risk is greater.

◊ If you start grooming your horse, clean its hooves, or saddle it, there is a risk that it does not stand still but starts moving around.

2. What can you do to reduce the risk?

◊ You must always tie up your horse before you start working with it. That is the only way to make sure that it stands still.

◊ Tie the horse in such a way that you have as much space around it as possible, for instance on a wide aisle way.

◊ When you work with the horse, stand to its side, not directly in front of it or directly behind it. If you stand in front of it, it can strike you with a front leg. If you stand behind it, it can strike you with a hind leg.

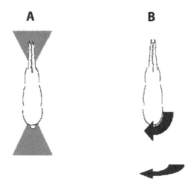

A. Avoid standing in the red zones.
B. When going around the horse
keep out of the reach of the hind legs
or keep very close to the back of the horse

◊ Stand as close to the horse as possible. If it should hit you with a kick, it will rather push you away instead of hammering its leg into you.

◊ Never stand right in front of or behind the horse. Stand to the side of it (A on the figure).

◊ When you need to go around the horse, either go as close to the horse as possible or as far away as possible, so that it cannot reach you with a front leg or a hind leg (B). If it should kick, it will not hurt you as badly if you are close to it as if you are a metre from it.

When you are close to a horse, you must either keep a sufficient distance from it, so that it cannot reach you if it should kick (that is especially true of other peoples' horses); or you should stand as close to the horse as possible, so that it only pushes you away if it should strike.

But you must only stand close to a horse if it is tied up or if you have a halter and lead rope on it.

You must never sit down on the ground close to a horse. If you do not want to bend down (for instance to brush its legs), you should kneel down so that you can jump up immediately if it should be necessary.

 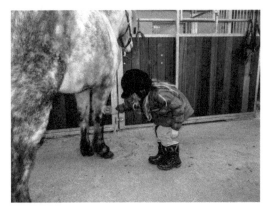

Touching a horse:

1. What is the risk?

    If you make a sudden move towards the horse it can become surprised and react by backing away, by biting or by kicking. Besides, many horses have places on them where they do not like to be touched, for instance around the ears. In addition, they can be ticklish so that a light touch will irritate them.

2. What can you do to reduce the risk?

    If you need to touch the horse a certain place, for instance down on one of the legs, start by touching them on a 'safe' place, for instance on the shoulder or the rump, and let your hand slide down along the leg. In that way the horse is less likely to kick (see also **Lifting a leg on a horse,** page 111).

    When you touch the horse, do it with a firm hand. If you touch it lightly, you might tickle it.

Brushing a horse:

1. What is the risk?

◊   When you brush a horse, be careful not to do it too hard, because it can irritate the horse, especially on places where bones are close to the skin (on legs, above the hip). This is particularly important when you use a hard brush.

◊   You also need to be aware that some horses can be ticklish, for instance in the groin. If so, the horse may kick out when it is brushed there.

2. What can you do to minimize the risk?

If there are areas on the horse where it does not want to be brushed, it is best to start brushing it somewhere else, where it does not mind it, and gradually work your way towards the sensitive area.

◊   Too much brushing is not good because it removes the oil from the hair, making it less water repellent. As a consequence, the horse is less protected against rain and wind.

◊   Too little brushing is not good, either. Dirt under the saddle or girth can irritate the horse and create sores. So a minimum of brushing to remove sand and mud is necessary before saddling the horse.

Lifting a leg on a horse:

1. What is the risk?

◊   When you reach out to lift a leg on your horse, there is a risk that it will strike out after your hand.

◊   When you have lifted a leg up, there is a risk that the horse tries to avoid it by kicking or putting weight on its leg.

◊   When you let go of the leg the horse may place it on top of your foot.

2. How can you prevent an accident?

◊   Before lifting your horse's leg you need to warn it about your intention. The best way to do so is to place your hand on its shoulder (if you want to lift a front leg) or on its rump (if you want to lift its hind leg). Thereafter, you let your hand glide down its leg till you reach the fetlock. Remember to have firm contact with the horse so you do not tickle it. Then, with your shoulder you push the weight of the horse over on the opposite leg, press forward on the fetlock till the horse bends its leg, where after you can lift it.

◊   While you keep the leg up you need a firm grip around the pastern so that the horse cannot pull its leg out of your hand.

◊   Remember to stand sufficiently to the side so that the horse does not step on you when you release the foot.

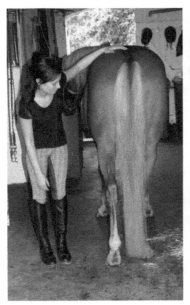 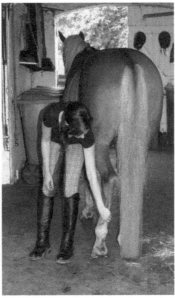 

1. Place your hand on the croup (for the hind leg) or shoulder (for the front leg)

2. Let the hand slide down with firm contact and push the weight of the horse onto the opposite leg

3. Lift the hoof

How do you lift a leg on a difficult horse?

◊   If a horse is unwilling to lift its legs, it can be helpful to put a rope around the pastern and to use the two ends of the rope as a kind of handle to lift the leg. It is important not to tie the rope around the leg. If the horse reacts strongly to having its legs touched so that the rope makes it react even more, of course this is not a good method. Instead you need to habituate it gradually to being touched. Start sufficiently high up on the horse so that it does not react. Work your hand down, for instance by rubbing the leg. If the horse reacts, move your hand up but do not let go of the contact until the horse has stopped reacting.

Cleaning the hooves on a horse:

1. What is the risk?

◊ Stones caught in the frog or small stones pressed up in the white line can make a horse lame or make it stumble during the ride. Cracks in the hoof wall can do the same.

◊ If your horse wears shoes, one of them can be loose, something that also can cause trouble on a ride.

2. How can you reduce the risk?

◊ It is important that you clean your horse's hooves, both before and after each ride. In that way you can ensure that there are no stones and that the shoes are sitting tightly.

Saddling a horse:

1. What is the risk?

◊ If the saddle is put on the horse with no warning, the horse can be surprised and react by jumping around.

◊ If you go away from the horse before the girth is fastened, the saddle can fall off. For one thing, this can scare the horse. For another, it can ruin the saddle.

◊ If the saddle cloth or numnah and the saddle are not placed correctly, it can irritate the horse and make it buck or something similar. Moreover, a misplaced saddle can cause saddle sores

◊   Some horses try to bite when a saddle is put on them.

◊   Some horses kick forward with a hind leg when the rider reaches out to take the girth.

◊   Some horses take a deep breath and hold the air while you tighten the girth, to prevent it from being tightened too much, a bad habit called bloating. If you are not aware of it, the girth may be too loose when you start riding.

2.   How can you avoid an accident?

◊   Before you place the saddle on the back of your horse, you need to warn it about it by touching its back or by showing it the saddle.

◊   Place saddle cloth or numnah and saddle on the withers of the horse and pull them back till they are on the right spot. In that way, the hairs in the coat will lie down smoothly under the saddle.

◊   Make sure you tighten the girth (maybe only just a little) right after you have ensured that the saddle pad or numnah and saddle are lying correctly.

◊   When you have placed the saddle on the horse from the left side, you need to go over on the other side to check that everything is lying as it should.

◊   Keep an eye on the head of the horse when you put the saddle on it. Be careful that nobody is standing too close to the horse at that moment because they could also get bitten.

◊   If your horse kicks out when you are reaching for the girth, yell at it. If necessary, you can pull the free end of the girth towards you with a whip or something similar.

◊   Besides making sure that the hairs are lying smoothly under the saddle, you also must make sure that the saddle cloth or numnah is lying smoothly without wrinkles (a)

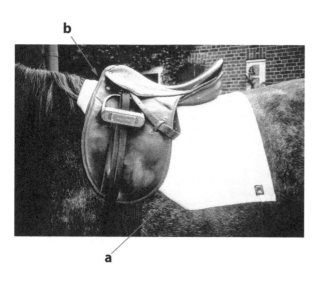

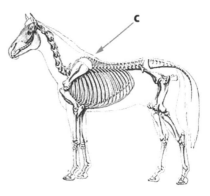

◊   and that it is pulled up into the gullet in front (b) so that it does not press down on the spine of the horse (c) and so that fresh air can come in between saddle and horse's back.

Tightening the girth:

◊   When you have placed the saddle on the horse, tighten the girth lightly. When you have checked on both sides of the horse that it is lying correctly, you can tighten the girth a little more. You must tighten it equally from both sides. Instead of tightening it two holes from one side, you should tighten it one hole on either side. If you only tighten the girth from one side you will pull the skin up which can irritate the horse.

◊   The final tightening of the girth you should not do until the horse has walked a short distance. If you tighten it before the horse has moved its front legs, the skin between elbows and girth can be 'too short' and irritate the horse.

◊   If you wish to tighten the girth completely, before the horse moves (for instance, because you use a Western saddle), you can lift, first, one leg, then the other, to loosen the skin around the elbow.

> **Do not forget to tighten the girth before you start riding. Otherwise the saddle can turn around with you, or it can cause saddle sores if it is lying too loose.**

Remember: The saddle must fit your horse. A poorly fitting saddle can cause pain or soreness in the horse's back and make it difficult or impossible to ride it. If your horse gains or loses weight, or if it is still in its growing phase, its saddle may no longer fit. If you are not able to judge yourself if the saddle fits your horse, get an experienced person to evaluate it.

(See also **Maintenance of the safety lock that carries the stirrup strap**, page 29).

Bridling a horse

◊　　As long as the horse is tied up with a halter and a rope, you can move away from it. When you have taken off the halter and bridled the horse, you cannot leave it, unless you ask somebody to hold the horse for you.

◊　　Therefore, it is important that you get the things you need for the ride (riding helmet, jacket, mobile phone, whip, etc.) *before* you bridle the horse.

◊　　So the sequence is: saddle the horse, get ready for the ride, and bridle the horse.

You must never tie up a horse with the reins. If it pulls back, the bit can damage its mouth.

1. What is the risk?

◊　　When you remove the halter from the horse, before getting the bridle on, there is a risk that the horse wanders off.

◊　　If you are standing in front of the horse while you put on its bridle, there is a risk that it lifts its head and bumps into your head or your stomach.

◊　　When you put the bit into its mouth, there is a risk that it bites you.

◊　　When you have placed the bridle on the horse, before you have buckled up the throatlatch and the noseband (cavesson), the buckles can hit you or the horse itself if it makes a sudden movement.

2. How can you avoid an accident?

◊   The safest way to bridle a horse is

1. to loosen the rope in the halter
2. to place the reins from the bridle around the front part of the neck of the horse
3. to take off the halter from the horse
4. to hold the bridle up in front of the horse's head, place the bit in its mouth, and put the head piece over its ears till it is in the right place
5. to check if the bit is lying straight in its mouth
6. to check if the browband is placed correctly
7. to place the noseband correctly and to buckle it
8. to buckle the throatlatch

◊   Some horses lift their head when the head piece is pulled over their ears. If the horse is tied up it may pull back when it feels resistance from the rope. Therefore, it is safest to untie the horse before the halter is removed from the horse.

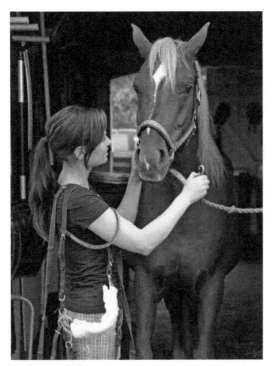

Untie the halter

Place the reins over the neck right behind the ears

Take off the halter

Put the bridle on the horse

◊   Remember to hang up the halter when you have taken it off so that it is not lying on the ground where the horse can step on it.

◊   Instead of loosening the rope in the halter and place the reins around the neck of the horse, you can unbuckle the neck piece of the halter and place it around its neck. When you have bridled the horse you then loosen the halter and remove it.

◊   You must always stand to the side of the horse when you bridle it so that it will not hit you in the head or stomach, should it lift its head.

◊   Put the bit into the mouth of the horse by having it lying in your open palm, as when you give your horse a treat. If the horse refuses to open its mouth, press with your thumb on the skin covering its jaw till it opens its mouth.

◊   If the horse has a habit of lifting its head when you bridle it, take hold of the cheek pieces of the bridle with your right hand and use that hand to hold down the head of the horse. With your left hand you then place the bit in the mouth of the horse.

When you have bridled your horse, check:

1. that the bit is lying correctly in the mouth

2. that the brow band is lying straight and does not irritate the horse's ears

3. that the noseband is lying correctly, that is not too far up and not too far down

4. that the throatlatch is not too tight

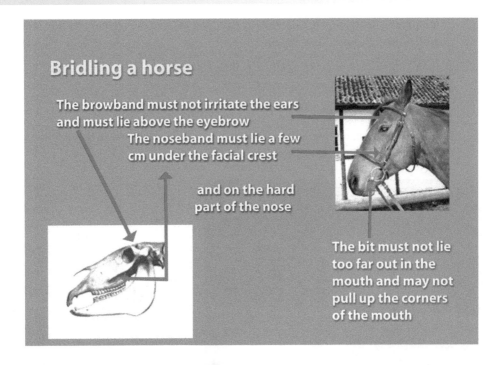

If the horse lifts its head as you put the bit in its mouth, hold down the head with the hand that holds the bridle.

Taking off the bridle:

1. What is the risk?

◊ When you unbuckle the buckles to take off the bridle, many horses try to scratch their head against you. It can be very uncomfortable to have bridle and buckles scraped against you.

◊ When you have taken off the bridle, before you get the halter on the horse, there is a risk that your horse goes away from you.

2. How can you avoid an accident?

◊ When the horse tries to rub itself against you, push it away and wait to unbuckle things until the horse is quiet. You should not allow your horse to develop that bad habit.

When you have unbuckled the throatlatch and noseband, you put the reins around the neck of the horse, right behind the ears, so that you can use the reins to stop the horse should it wander off. Then you pull the head piece over the ears and lower the bridle so that the horse lets go of the bit. Thereafter, you put the halter on the horse and remove the reins. In the end you fasten a rope to the halter.

Place the reins over the neck right behind the ears.

Take off the bridle. If necessary hold on to the reins.

Put the halter on the horse.

Take the reins from the neck.

Tie the horse.

Leading a horse through a door:

1. What is the risk?

◊   When you lead a horse through a relatively narrow door or gate opening, the horse may push its way through before you, so that you get crushed.

◊   If you go in front of the horse through the door, the horse may step on your heels.

◊   If the horse has a saddle on, the saddle or the stirrups may get stuck in a door handle or something.

◊   If the door is opening out towards you, the wind may close it as you are walking through and hit the horse. That can scare the horse so that it jumps forward and into you.

2. How can you avoid an accident?

◊   When you lead a horse up to a door, stop it before you go through the door (see **Teaching**

the horse to stop, page 69). When it stands still, take a step forward and give it the command to go forward (see **Teaching the horse to go forward,** page 68) but at a speed so that it keeps a distance to you.

◊ Make sure that the door opening is wide enough to allow horse and saddle through and keep a distance to the sides so that the saddle does not bump into the door frame.

◊ If the door cannot stay open by itself (for instance because of the wind) make sure that it is fastened with a hook or a rope or something, or ask somebody to keep it open for you.

◊ Make sure the stirrups are run up on the straps so that they are not hanging down. In that way they are less likely to get caught in door handles and similar things.

Leading a horse into its stable:

1. What is the risk?

If you remove the lead rope from the horse in the aisle way to let it go in by itself, there is a risk that it does not go in but goes somewhere else. If it is eager to get into its stable (for instance because there is feed in its food trough), it may rush in and hurt itself on the door frame. If you lead it into the stable and let it loose, it may step on you or squeeze you against the wall while turning around.

2.   How can you avoid an accident?

Lead your horse up to the stable door and give it a signal to stop (see **Teaching the horse to stop,** page 69). When you have opened the door, give it a signal to go behind you into the stable (see To teach the horse to go forward). When both of you are all the way in, turn the horse around so it faces the doorway and give it a signal to stop. Take off the lead rope and leave the stall.

Passing other horses in the aisle way:

1.   What is the risk?

In stables where horses are tied up in the aisle way between two rows of stables, it often happens that another horse needs to pass to get out. Unless the aisle way is very wide it means that the two horses get close to one another. If the two horses are not the best of friends, they may start fighting, one horse trying to bite or kick the other. If the tied up horse is tied with two ropes to either side of the aisle way, it is necessary to untie one rope to let the horse pass. This may cause the tied horse to turn around a little so that it blocks the whole aisle way. Obviously, the risk of an accident is greater in that situation.

2.   How can you avoid an accident?

A horse should not be left unattended tied up in the aisle way. Consequently, there should be a person in the vicinity that you can ask for help getting out your horse. Wait with your horse till the helper has loosened one rope and moved the horse sufficiently to the side, so that you can pass. The helper should remain by the head of the tied up horse so that she can intervene if it should lay back its ears or otherwise show signs of aggression.

If nobody is around to help you, do not try to pass the tied up horse. Instead, lead your horse into an empty stable and put the other horse into its own stable before going out with your own horse.

3.   What should you do if the two horses start fighting?

Obviously, if the two horses start kicking out after each other, make sure you are out of reach. If necessary, let go of your horse and stand back in order not to get kicked.

Mucking out:

1. What is the risk?

    If you muck out a stable with a loose horse in it, it is likely to be in the way. You cannot keep an eye on the horse and do the job at the same time. If you park the wheelbarrow in the door opening the horse may try to push its way out past it. If you stand the fork against the wall while you take the wheelbarrow out to empty it, a curious horse may push the fork over and get hurt on it.

2. What should you do to reduce the risk?

    It is a bad idea to clean a stable, to spread straw, and to sweep the aisle way with horses around. Ammonia and dust are bad for them. Before you start the work, take the horse out of the stable, preferably out to the pasture together with other horses.

    In general, remember to keep the stable orderly. Hang up tools and put away equipment so that it does not lay around in the aisle way and other places. Not only can the things get ruined, but the horses may also step on them and get their feet tangled up in them, which can make them spook.

Chapter 9

Riding

Mounting a horse:

1. What is the risk?

   When you mount a horse it is important that it stands still while you do it.
   It must stand still while you put your foot in the stirrup.
   It must stand still while you swing your right leg up over its back.
   It must stand still while you adjust the stirrups.
   It must stand still until you give it the command to go forward.

   Remember:
   You are the one to decide what the horse
   should do and what it should not do

   If it does not stand still while you stand with one leg on the ground and the other in the stirrup, you can lose your balance if the horse moves forward.

   If you adjust the stirrups after you have mounted, you may not have complete control over the horse if it starts walking off on its own. If there are other horses nearby, you may get too close to them so that they start kicking each other.

   But the most important reason why your horse must stand still is that you are the one to decide when it can go forward, not the horse.

   If you mount the horse without first checking that the girth is tight enough to carry your weight, the saddle may turn around while you are mounting.

When you stand with your left leg in the stirrup and your right leg on the ground, you put a lot of weight on the side of the horse. If the girth is not sufficiently tight, the saddle can be pulled down so that it is no longer lying straight. It can be very uncomfortable for the horse to be pulled sideways every time a rider mounts it.

2. How can you avoid the problems?

Before you put your foot in the stirrup you collect both reins in your left hand so that you have contact with the horse's mouth. To have contact with its mouth means that you are able to feel just a slight tension on the reins. At the same time you place your left hand on the upper front part of the saddle so that you can avoid pulling it in its mouth while you mount it.

If the horse starts moving forward you release your hold of the saddle and pull back the reins till the horse stands still. This procedure you need to follow every time the horse moves forward, no matter how far up on the horse you are. Remember to release the pressure when it stands still

If your horse is very difficult to hold back you need somebody to hold it while you mount it, at least in the beginning.

Remember to check that the girth is sufficiently tight before you mount the horse.

By using a mounting block when you mount the horse, you avoid pulling the saddle crooked and you make it less uncomfortable for the horse. It means, however, that the horse must learn to stand still next to the mounting block, which is something it has to be trained to do (see **Training your horse to stand still next to a mounting block,** page 76).

3. What should you do if you cannot stop the horse?

◊   If the horse is on its way over to some other horses or towards a place where it is unsafe to be, you have to stop whatever you are doing (mounting, stirrup adjustment) and concentrate on controlling the horse and make it stop.

◊   Before you start the actual ride, after you have warmed up your horse, check the girth once more. If the saddle is too loose it can cause saddle sores. If the girth is very loose, the saddle can turn around during the ride.

1. Shorten the reins so that you have a light contact with the mouth.

2. If the horse starts walking stop it immediately by pulling the reins.

3. Continue to mount when the horse has stopped.

Dismounting from a horse:

1. What is the risk?

> If you dismount from a horse by keeping one foot in the stirrup you can lose your balance if the horse should move forward while you stand with only one foot on the ground.

> If you wear a safety vest, it may get stuck on the saddle as you are sliding down. In the worst case you may fall under the horse.

2. How can you avoid it?

> Before you swing your right leg over the back of the horse, you take both feet out of the stirrups, so that you can land on both feet. Push yourself a little away from the horse as you jump down.

Warming up a horse:

1. What is the risk?

A horse that has been standing still for some time has a reduced blood circulation. Consequently, its muscles do not work as well as when the heart rate is higher. In addition, the production of fluid in the joints is also reduced. Both states are more pronounced in cold weather. The risk that the horse stumbles is greater.

But it is not only the work capacity of the horse that is reduced in the beginning; that of the rider is also reduced. The rider must also be prepared for the ride, both physically and psychologically. Physically, your muscles and joints must perform. And psychologically you must concentrate on the horse and the ride.

2. How can you avoid an accident?

When you start to ride it is important to ride quietly in walk or trot for the first 10 minutes or so. If the warm-up is done on loose reins, the horse has a better chance to stretch its neck.

Before starting the actual ride, it is a good idea to repeat the 'basic rules' that you are the one to give the commands and the horse is the one to obey them. A good way to do so is to spend a few minutes on the exercises described in the section: **Training from the ground,** page 68. Make the horse go forward a few steps by giving a light pull forward with the reins. Stop the horse by giving a light pull backwards with the reins. Make it go a few steps backwards by putting backwards pressure on the reins. For one thing, you repeat what the horse (hopefully) has learned earlier. For another, you remind the horse about who gives the commands and who follows them. And thirdly, you remind the horse to react to light pressure.

Riding with loose reins:

A very effective way to reward a horse during the ride is to give it a break. The best way to do so is to give it loose reins. In that way it can stretch its neck and give its neck muscles a chance to relax.

If the horse is excited about something it is also a good idea to make it calm down by giving it loose reins. The opportunity to stretch its neck and lower its head makes it calm down faster.

Many riders are afraid of riding their horse with loose reins because they feel that they do not have any control over their horse. They are afraid that it will run off.

1. What is the risk?

   When you ride with loose reins the horse may suddenly charge, especially if it gets scared of something. Before the rider gets hold of the reins, the horse may be running wildly and, therefore, hard to stop.

2. What should you do to avoid the situation?

   The safest way to ride with loose reins is to hold the reins with one hand (left hand if you are right handed) on the middle of the reins (that is, by the buckle).

   If the horse starts running you pull your left hand towards you, grasp with your right hand around both reins, and continue the pressure on the reins till the horse has stopped again.

   In that way you have just as much control over the horse and you can react just as fast as when you ride with shorter reins.

3. What should you do if the horse runs off?

   See **Stopping a horse that is bolting** (page 155).

Hold the reins with one hand   **If the horse starts running...**

...pull with the hand, grab both reins with the other hand and continue pulling...

...till the horse stops.

Collecting a horse:

Approximately two thirds of the horse's weight is carried by the front legs. When the horse has a rider on its back, two thirds of the rider's weight is also carried by the front legs. The purpose of collecting a horse is to get its hind legs closer to the point of gravity so that a larger part of the weight of horse and rider is carried by the hind legs. The front legs remain perpendicular while the hind legs step somewhat further in under the horse and the hind quarters are slightly lowered. The change in the weight distribution makes it easier for the horse to move. The degree of collection depends on what kind of movements the horse should make. Advanced dressage demands a higher degree of collection than hacking. Some horses are predisposed for a higher degree of collection (for instance modern breeds are less capable than baroque breeds such as Lusitanos and Lipizzaners). True collection can only be obtained after extensive training, riding simple exercises that increase suppleness, inducing mainly the inner hind leg to come increasingly under the body (circles, gait transitions, shoulder-in), so that the horse goes relaxed and in rhythm.

1. What is the risk?

    Many riders believe wrongly that collection of a horse is achieved by pulling on the reins and at the same time driving the horse forward with legs or seat. Similarly, it is a common mistake to believe that collection means bending the neck of the horse and lowering its head by means of the reins. When the horse is exposed simultaneously to two opposite commands (to stop because of rein pressure and to go forward because of leg pressure), it is experiencing a conflict that can make it buck, rear, or jump sideways. It is showing avoidance or conflict behaviour.

    If the horse is ridden with a lot of tension on the reins for a longer period of time without the rider releasing the tension, the horse will habituate to the pressure from the bit with the result that it will not stop when the rider pulls on the reins. The horse is what some riders incorrectly call 'hard in the mouth'.

If the head of the horse is forced down and backwards, so that its nose is behind the vertical line, it is only able to see a short distance ahead. Bumps on the ground can make it stumble and objects that suddenly appear in its field of vision may scare the horse.

2. How can you reduce the risk?

    When the horse starts to go collected during the initial training, as described above, the degree of collection may gradually be increased, first, by driving the horse forward (with slight pressure from seat and legs) and then to stop it a little with slight tension on the reins, so that it brings its hind legs further forward under its body. It is important that the two signals (legs and reins) are given with a fraction of a second apart, so that the horse does not experience a conflict.

    It is further important that the signal from the reins makes the horse slow down a little and that its reaction is reinforced by a release of the tension (see **Negative reinforcement, page 55**). In that way, you avoid that the horse stops reacting correctly to the rein pressure, that is, that it becomes 'hard in the mouth'.

    You must realize that the posture of the horse's head and neck is a result of the fact that its hind legs step further in under its body, not the other way around. It is not its bent neck that results in collection.

    Particularly when riding outdoors it is important to give the horse the opportunity to orient itself, that is, to give it the freedom to look around at the surroundings. If the horse has the opportunity to look at things from some distance, it is less likely to get scared.

    Putting tension on the reins is a signal to the horse to slow down or to stop. Therefore, the signal from the reins must never be used for anything else, such as to get it into a certain posture, because it will ruin the stopping effect of the reins. (See also **Signals, page 65**).

Falling off a horse:

1. What is the risk?

    The rider who has never fallen off a horse probably does not exist. It is (almost) impossible to be an active rider without falling off a horse. In most cases, luckily, nothing happens. The rider does not get hurt. Nevertheless, an unplanned dismount is risky. You must do what you can to avoid a fall from the horse.

    Of course, it is impossible to mention all the things that can happen if you fall off a horse. Apart from breaking arms or legs, the horse may step on you or kick you.

Apart from you getting hurt, your horse may also have an accident if it gets loose or otherwise causes an accident.

2.   What can you do to avoid getting hurt?

Besides trying to stay in the saddle (see for instance **Riding a horse that bucks,** page 167, and **Riding a horse that rears,** page 165), you must get your feet out of the stirrups and push away from the horse. Do not try to break the fall with your arms but try to roll away from the horse as soon as you hit the ground (which, of course, is easier said than done!).

Maybe you have learned that you must hold on to the reins when you have fallen off the horse. Of course, it makes sense when you are riding outdoors. Then maybe you do not have to walk home. But for one thing, it may not be the first thing you think of while you are falling. For another, it can actually be dangerous if the horse is charging. And also in this situation your own safety is at the top of the list.

Teaching a horse to stop when the rider has fallen off:

1.   What is the risk?

Obviously, a horse whose rider has fallen off and no longer has control over it constitutes a danger for others, both indoors and outdoors.

2.   What can you do to reduce the risk?

Besides the many pieces of advice described in other places in this book, it may be a good idea to teach the horse to stop when the rider has fallen off. The training should be done in an enclosed area, such as an indoor arena. First, you teach the horse to stop on command (for instance 'whoa'). Lead the horse forward, give the command and thereafter the rein signal to stop (light tension backwards). Reward it with a treat. When the horse has learned to stop on the command alone, without the rein signal, you may ride it around, first in walk, later in trot. While you are riding you jump off the horse (and at the same time you practice to land on your feet). Immediately when you touch ground, you give the command to stop. By regularly repeating the exercise, the horse will start to stop on its own when you have jumped off.

How you can avoid getting your foot stuck in a stirrup: see under Equipment: Safety stirrups.

How you teach your horse not to get scared when something is dragging behind it: see under **Training your horse to pull things behind it** (page 78).

Jumping off a horse

As the horse is trotting along...

...let go of reins and stirrups.

Place your hands on the withers or on the saddle and swing your legs up...

...and land on your feet.

Riding with spurs:

The purpose of using spurs is to support and localize the effect of the legs on the side of the horse so that the signal from the legs is as clear and as exact as possible (for instance whether the horse should increase the speed, transit into canter or yield to the leg). Spurs should not be used to punish the horse, for instance if it does not want to go forward.

An important requirement for using spurs is that the rider has perfect control over his or her legs and knows how to use the spurs on the horse. Spurs are not for beginners.

When you ride with spurs your feet must point straight forward, that is they must be parallel with the side of the horse, so that the spurs do not irritate the horse. When you use the spurs you then turn the toes slightly outwards so that the spurs work on the side of the horse.

If you train your horse in the right way to respond correctly to leg pressure (see **Teaching the horse to go forward,** page 71), you do not need spurs to make it go forward.

1. What is the risk?

   If you stumble you can hurt yourself wearing spurs.

   If the horse walks behind you and gets too close to you, it can step on the spurs so that you fall.

2. How can you reduce the risk?

   If you are of the opinion that spurs are a necessary part of your riding equipment, you need to put them on right before you mount the horse, and you need to take them off as soon as you have dismounted the horse. You should only wear spurs while you are actually sitting on the horse.

   It is a bad habit to walk around wearing spurs when you are not riding.

Riding with draw reins:

The purpose of using draw reins is to force the head and neck of the horse down. Because it is possible to exert a very strong pressure on the mouth and head of the horse, draw reins should only be used by experienced riders and only for the retraining of horses with specific problems.

It is not unusual to see riders using draw reins during the warm up period before riding a competition. If the horse has been trained correctly, it should not be necessary to subject it to that kind of treatment.

Some riders use draw reins in a misunderstood attempt to achieve collection of their horse. Collection is achieved through correct riding (see **Collecting a horse,** page 131), not by forcing its head down.

Riding with a martingale

◊ The purpose of using a martingale is to prevent the horse from raising its head and neck so high that it actually hits the rider. A martingale should be adjusted so that it does not affect the horse as long as it keeps its head in a normal position. Only if it raises its head above a certain level should the martingale force the horse's head and neck down. If a horse throws its head up and down, however, the behaviour could be an indication that it feels some kind of discomfort (toothache, back problems etc.) that needs to be checked.

◊   Some riders use a martingale that is too tight in an attempt to force the horse's head down, again in a misunderstood attempt to achieve collection. It is wrong to use a martingale in this way. Collection is achieved by correct riding (see **Collecting a horse,** page 131), not by force.

◊   In general, the use of this and similar 'aids' can help the training of a horse, especially a 'problem' horse, if used correctly. But they can cause much damage if used incorrectly. It is important that the rider understands what correct (and incorrect) use means, before using these aids. They are certainly not for beginners but should only be used by experienced riders.To use aids to compensate for poor riding skills does not only mean that rider and horse may never be able to function together in harmony. The biggest problem is, however, that the horse may react against these kinds of restraint and develop behaviour problems that can make riding it dangerous.

Above left: incorrect use of draw reins.   Above right: correct use of a martingale.

> **Incorrect use of various aids can result in the horse developing behaviour problems.**
> **If this happens the horse may become useless because it will be too dangerous to ride.**

Riding with a sharp bit:

1.   What is the risk?

◊   That a bit is sharp means that it is painful for the horse if the rider pulls hard on the reins. A sharp bit can either be a thin snaffle bit, a curb bit or a three-ring bit. Used incorrectly, the horse may react strongly, for instance by lifting its head as a reaction to the pain. If you are riding outdoors and your horse is cantering too fast for your liking, a dangerous situation may happen if it lifts its head because the horse may not see where it is going.

    2.   What should you do to reduce the risk?

◊   In principle, there is nothing wrong in using a sharp bit, as long as it is used correctly. For one thing, you should only use very light rein aid such as a slight tightening of your fingers which means that you must have good control over your hands. For another, it is extremely important that you release the pressure (that is, tension on the reins) at the right moment, that is, as soon as the horse slows down or stops (see **Negative reinforcement,** page 55)

◊   If a horse does not react correctly to the pressure from the bit, it usually means that the rider has attempted to get it to go in a certain position with its head and neck by pulling on the reins (see **Collecting a horse,** page 131). If the rein signal is not followed by 1. the horse slowing down and 2. a release of the pressure as a reinforcement , the rein signal loses its stopping effect because the horse habituates to the constant pressure. The horse 'loses its brakes'.

An example of a sharp bit

Riding an unknown horse:

Before sitting on a horse that you do not know, you should get to know it to some extent.

Statistics show that relatively speaking, more accidents happen when the rider rides an unknown horse. The first couple of times you ride it, you should only ride it in an indoor arena or a fenced in riding arena. An exception to that advice is the horse in the riding school where it is the job of the riding instructor to make sure that the horse you ride fits your level.

A good way to get to know a horse is to start by grooming and saddling it and, if possible, to ask people who know the horse. In addition, you can lead the horse around, stop it and let it stand still for a short time, that is, to do some of the exercises described under **Basic training: Training from the ground,** page 68.

Unless you are an experienced rider you should first lead the horse out in the countryside to find out how it reacts to traffic and other outdoor things. In other words, take a walk in the woods with the horse, before you ride it out. If the horse gets scared of certain things, it is usually safer to find out walking beside it than sitting on its back. It is, however, a prerequisite that the horse has learned to walk calmly next to the rider.

The purpose of doing these exercises first is not only to get to know the horse. The purpose is just as much the opposite, that the horse gets to know you. If it learns from the very beginning that you are the one to give the commands and that it has to obey the commands, it is much more likely to behave correctly. If you are able to convey to the horse who the leader is, in a decisive and consistent yet confidence-creating way, the horse is much more likely to obey you and to trust you.

Riding an energetic horse:

1. What is the risk?

   A horse that has been standing in its stable for a longer period can be difficult to ride, especially if you ride it outdoors. Either it may be happy finally to get out or, if it has been standing in a very quiet environment, it may react strongly to sounds and things that move.

2. What can you do to reduce the risk?

   The best way to avoid an accident is to turn the horse out in the pasture, preferably together with other horses, so that it can get rid of some of its energy and get used to things happening around it.

   Another possibility is to lunge the horse. If it should start to buck it is safer to stand on the ground than to sit on its back. Most horses will show their playfulness when they start trotting or cantering. Remember first to warm up the horse by letting them walk around, especially in cold weather.

You need to lunge the horse for a sufficiently long time to get rid of its excess energy. Unless it is in very good shape lungeing for 15 minutes is usually enough.

When a horse is playful it shows it by lifting and shaking its head while it makes smaller bucks. If your horse shows these signs after you have started riding it, there is a risk that it continues by making larger bucks. You can prevent this development by distracting the horse. Slow down to a walk and ask it to do various exercises, such as leg-yielding, making a volte (small circle) or something similar, so that its attention is diverted to something else.

Riding two on a horse:

1. What is the risk?

   The fact that a horse is used to carry one person on its back does not necessarily mean that it will allow two people to sit there. Many horses are sensitive on their rump which means that a touch or pressure in that area may cause it to buck or to kick out with its hind legs. But also non-sensitive horses may react to the extra weight.

2. How can you reduce the risk?

   If it for some reason is necessary that your horse must be able to carry two riders, it has to be trained to do so. The adaptation can be done in the same way that you train a young horse, which means that rider number two more or less proceeds as described under Starting a young horse.

Leading a pack horse:

When you go trekking it may be necessary to bring a pack horse that can carry some of the luggage. But also in other situations it may be necessary to lead a second horse. If you are out hacking and one of the other riders for some reason cannot continue the ride, it may be necessary to bring the horse home. Furthermore, if you want to let your young child come along on the ride, you may want to have a rope on the child's pony.

1. What is the risk?

   To stop a horse running wild can be difficult. To stop two horses running wild can be impossible. When two or more horses run in a group, they tend to agitate each other which makes it even more difficult to stop them. And to let go of the hand-held horse is a bad solution if you are out in the country.

If the two horses do not know each other or if they do not get along, problems may arise if they start fighting during the ride.

2.   How can you reduce the risk?

The handheld horse must learn to go next to the ridden horse (and vice versa). Start the training in a fenced in area, so that you can let go of the hand horse, should it be necessary. Teach the handheld horse to stop and to go forward on command from the lead rope (see Training from the ground). If necessary, train in all three gaits.

Even though you do not plan to lead a second horse while riding, it is a good idea to train it in the riding arena, so that the horse is reasonably used to the situation should it become necessary.

Chapter 10

Riding in the arena

Going into an indoor arena:

1. What is the risk?

   Whether you have to open a door or you can go straight through an opening, horses that are already in the arena can get scared, if somebody enters without warning. A door that opens into the hall can hit a horse going by. The sound of the door slamming can frighten a horse.

   Trying to open the door while sitting on your horse can be risky if you do not get it sufficiently open, or if the door closes by itself while you are going through.

2. How can you reduce the risk?

   You must always warn other riders that you are coming in (for instance 'door free!') and wait for the answer that you can come in. If you do it in that way it is not just the riders that are warned about the door being opened. The horses are warned, too.

   Unless a horse is specially trained to stand still while you open the door, you should get off the horse to go through. But also, when you lead the horse through the door, you have to be careful that the door does not close by itself.

Knowing the 'traffic rules' in the riding arena:

1. What is the risk?

   When several riders use the riding arena it is important not to get too close to each other. For one thing, a horse may kick and hit the other horse or its rider. For another, when riding in opposite directions, the riders can bump their knees together if there is not enough distance between them.

2. How can you avoid an accident?

It is important always to keep an eye on whereabouts in the arena the other riders are. You must never be so concentrated on your riding that you do not notice what is going on around you.

You should always turn your horse towards a place where there are fewest riders. If everybody does that, you will be equally spread out over the arena.

Riders riding in opposite directions should pass left of each other and with sufficient distance.

If one rider rides along the track and another on the circle, the latter must yield to the former by making the circle somewhat smaller.

Mounting, dismounting, and breaks should be done in the middle of the arena so that the passage along the track and on the circles is free for the other riders.

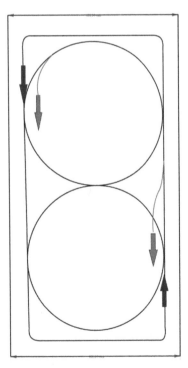

When riding in opposite directions, pass left of each other.

When riding on the circle, yield to riders along the track.

When standing still, do it in the middle of one of the circles.

Frightening other horses in the riding arena

1. What is the risk?

    A horse that is excited and tends to run fast in the riding arena can frighten other horses and make them run fast. If there are young horses or less experienced riders in the arena, this situation can be unpleasant and dangerous for the other riders.

    The same situation can happen if you are lungeing your horse. If it suddenly runs fast and maybe also bucks, its excitement can spread very fast to other horses.

2. How can you reduce the risk?

    If you suspect that your horse will show this kind of behaviour, you either have to wait till you are alone or at least ask permission from the other riders to lunge your horse or to ride your excited horse.

Lungeing a horse:

1. What is the risk?

    The further away you are from your horse, the less control you have over it. The less control you have over your horse, the greater the risk that it will become 'independent' and, for instance, try to run away or to buck. If the horse is playful, it may try to kick out in your direction.

2. How can you reduce the risk?

    Start the lungeing by leading the horse around on a circle while you walk at the level of its shoulder. Thereafter, you gradually increase the distance to the horse, in that you approach the middle of the circle. If the horse tries to run forward, stop it with the lunge line. If it stops, drive it quietly forward with the lunge whip. After a couple of rounds, you can get the horse to trot.

3. What should you do if the horse acts up?

If the horse at some point starts running too fast or begins bucking, you must stop it immediately with the lunge line by pulling it towards you in the middle. On a small circle it cannot run fast. You should not allow it to decide for itself how fast it may go.

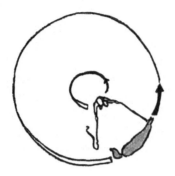

Chapter 11

Riding outdoors

◊   Riding outdoors (hacking) is more difficult than riding in the arena for many reasons.

◊   The risk of surprises is greater: loose dogs, wildlife fleeing, people with baby buggies, umbrellas or backpacks, machines making funny sounds, and numerous other things.

◊   To ride out 'in real life' obviously demands much more of both horse and rider.

◊   In this section some of the things that can constitute a risk are described. As mentioned in the chapter **Training the horse to be safe** (page 52), it is a good idea to habituate your horse to some of the situations that we know can scare a horse. But obviously it is not possible to habituate them to all the different things that can happen during an outdoor ride.

◊   We cannot teach a horse not to get scared. We can, however, to some extent teach it not to flee if it gets scared. Apart from reducing the flight behaviour of the horse, the training has two other effects.

◊   First of all, it provides you with a lot of information about your horse. You find out how your horse reacts when it is wary of something or when it gets scared. And this knowledge can help you to react in a more effective way when something happens.

◊   Secondly, your horse learns that the signals and the reactions that you (hopefully) have taught it during the basic training (especially to stop when you tighten the reins), also apply when the horse feels insecure or frightened.

◊   To how many different things a horse must be habituated depends on its temperament. But as you are training your horse you will be able to see that it reacts less and less when you try out something new. In that way, you will know when to expect that your horse remains relatively calm when it meets something new and unknown.

> **When you ride outdoors you should never ride alone. The safest is to ride out together with other people.**

> **Before you ride outdoors, you should tell somebody where you are going and when you will be back, so that he or she can react, if you are not back as planned.**

◊ As described in the section **Riding ability** (page 22) it is important that, when several riders are riding cross country, it is the least experienced rider who sets the tempo. The more experienced riders must not ride in such a way (ride faster, jump obstacles, or the like) that the less experienced rider cannot manage. The more experienced riders must consider the ability of the less experienced rider so that everybody has a positive experience.

◊ But when all the precautions have been listed, it is important to realize that, riding down a path in the woods is a healing thing, both for the rider and for the horse. Also a dressage champion horse that is mostly ridden in the arena needs some relaxation and variation in its daily rides.

Riding outdoors in a group:

1. What is the risk?

   When two or more horses are out on a tour together, it sometimes feels as if they start to compete with each other, especially in the faster gaits. If that happens they can be difficult to control.

   If a horse goes too close to the horse in front of it, both horse and rider cannot see where they are going. The risk that the horse stumbles over something on the ground is greater. The risk that the rider bumps into a low hanging branch or something is greater. Obviously, there is also a risk that the horse in front kicks the horse behind, and that it hits its rider instead of the horse. The same risk exists when the two riders ride side by side.

   If you ride in mud or on gravel, the horses in front of you may kick up mud or stones and hit the horses and riders behind them which is not only unpleasant but can also hurt.

2. How can you reduce the risk?

   Before you go out on a ride together, you should make a trial run in the riding arena, all of you riding around in canter as a group. For one thing, the horses may get used to cantering together. For another, you may identify horses that have problems with that kind of riding, so that you can habituate them somewhat more to the situation.

It is always important to keep your distance when riding behind another horse. Outdoors, it is especially important to keep sufficient distance so that both horse and rider can see what lies ahead of them. Horses that push forward into the horse in front must learn to keep a distance, or maybe you need to let them go in front. But also when you ride side by side, it is important to keep sufficient distance.

Keep at least one horse length distance; in a fast canter even more than that. The front rider needs to signal any change in speed. The usual way is to say 'trot' or 'canter' when changing to a faster gait, and to raise one arm when slowing down. In a large group the commands must be repeated down the line, so that the last riders also get the message.

If the ground is 'loose', that is, muddy or stony, it is important to keep extra distance and to avoid riding too close to each other.

3. What should you do if an accident happens?

    If one of the horses in the group is running uncontrolled, the only thing the other riders can do is to stop. When the run-away horse realises that the group is not following, it is more prone to stop. The rider of the horse may try to stop it, as described in the section **Stopping a horse that is bolting** page 155).

Riding past scary things:

◊   When a horse approaches something that makes it suspicious, it will focus all of its attention on the place. Its ears will be directed forward, it will lift its head to get the object directly into focus, and it will probably start slowing down, possibly stopping altogether, or try to go around the object. If the place or the object is very frightening, it may try to turn around and run away.

◊   If you drive the horse forward and force it to stay on course, it may resist even more.

1. What is the risk?

◊   When a horse is forced to go forward towards something that scares it and makes it unsafe, the probability that it will resist is great. It may turn around and run in the opposite direction or, if it is prevented from turning around, it may rear.

2. How can you prevent the situation?

◊   The reaction of the horse (to turn around or to rear) depends upon how forcefully you drive it forward.

◊   Therefore, you must be patient and only drive it forwards to the extent that it remains calm. The more you permit the horse to look at the object, the greater the chance that its curiosity wins over its fright. Remember to give it freedom to stretch its neck (see **Riding with loose reins,** page 129).

◊   If that is not enough to get the horse to go by the place, you can try to ride around it in a half circle that is big enough so that the horse is far enough away to still feel reasonably safe. You may even habituate the horse to the place or the object by turning around and going back, also in a half circle, but this time a little bit closer. If you repeat going back and forth with less and less distance, the horse may eventually get used to the place.

◊   If the horse is very excited, it may be necessary to dismount it and lead it instead of riding it. If it trusts you, your presence (preferably between the horse and the object!) can have a calming effect.

◊   Some horses are less afraid if the rider goes in front towards the place so that it can 'hide' behind the person. If that is the case with your horse, you may try that approach.

◊   Having a more experienced (and not scared) horse go in front may also make the approach easier.

> **Some horses can be more difficult to hold when you are standing on the ground than when you sit in the saddle. Therefore, you should only get off if you are afraid of falling off the horse or if you know that that will calm it down.**

Riding in a strong wind:

1. What is the risk?

As described under **Horses' vision** (page 32) horses see best things that move. When the wind blows a lot of things move, something that may make it tense. It may not react to the movements but it makes it tense and more likely to react if something else happens. It may not react to the branches blowing in the wind, but if a plastic bag suddenly comes flying, it is much more likely to turn around and flee.

2.   How can you avoid a problem?

When you are riding in a strong wind you must be extra careful and extra ready to react if your horse should suddenly show flight behaviour. Keep an eye on the surroundings, sit deep in the saddle, press your knees together, and be prepared to stop your horse before it starts to run (see **Riding with loose reins,** page 129).

Riding in traffic:

1.   What is the risk?

◊   Considering that horses have an innate motivation to flee from anything that chases after them, it is no wonder that they can become scared when a car, a truck, a bus, or a tractor drives towards them.

◊   If a horse has not learned that traffic is not dangerous, it will react by fleeing. The risk that it creates an accident is great.

◊   Not only can horse or rider be seriously hurt; other people using the road can, too.

2.   How can you prevent an accident?

◊   If you do not know whether your horse is traffic-safe, you have to find out before going out in traffic. You can do so by leading or riding it some distance from a less busy road, preferably a road where the cars are not driving fast.

◊   If you are together with a traffic-experienced horse, this can have a calming effect on your horse.

◊   Remember that even if your horse is not afraid of cars, it may still be frightened by trucks, motorcycles, tractors, or trains.

◊   In the chapter **Training the horse to be safe** (page 52), you can read about how to habituate your horse to motorcycles or tractors.

3. What should you do if a dangerous situation happens?

◊   If you are riding down a road and you see a big harvester or some other scary vehicle drive towards you, try to ride as far away from the road as possible. If there is a side road or an open piece of land nearby, go in that way.

◊   Turn the horse towards the vehicle so that it can see it as clearly as possible.

◊   Keep your horse moving. In frightening situations it is difficult for a horse to stand still.

◊   If you can get the attention of the driver, give him a signal to slow down so that he is aware that you have a problem with your horse.

Crossing a road as a group:

1. What is the risk?

◊   Many horses have a hard time standing still when they feel unsafe. To stand still at the side of a road and wait for a pause in the traffic can be very difficult for some horses.

◊   If there are two or more riders that have to cross the road it can sometimes be difficult to get across as a group. Horses left behind can become very excited and try to follow after the horses that got across. Obviously, this can create a very dangerous situation.

> **Make sure that you cross a road together as a group so that no horse is left behind**

Horses that are left behind on one side of the road can get very excited and try to run after the horses that got across, which can be extremely dangerous.

2. How can you avoid the situation?

◊   If your horse has a difficult time standing still while you are waiting, let it walk along the road until you can get across. If there is enough space you can also ride around in a small circle next to the road.

◊   If you are riding in a group and you all need to cross a road, ride in a single file along the road. When there is a pause in the traffic you all turn left and cross the road simultaneously. When you reach the other side you again form a single file and ride back to the level where you started. In this way, the crossing does not take more time than when a single rider goes across.

     1. Turn down the road you want to cross and ride in a single file along the road
     2. When all riders are riding along the road and when there is a pause in the traffic…
     3. …you cross the road simultaneously
     4. and again ride in a single file back along the road you crossed till you can turn down the way you wanted to go

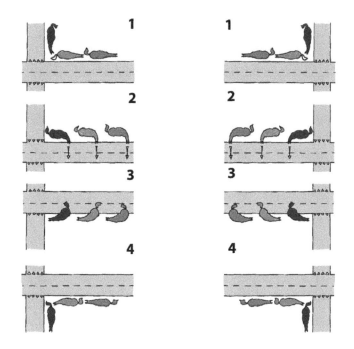

Above left: crossing the road in countries that drive on the left hand side. Above right: crossing the road in countries that drive on the right hand side.

3. What can you do if a problematic situation occurs?

◊ If your horse becomes so excited that you cannot control it, you can dismount if you know that that will calm it down. Remember that an excited horse can be more difficult to control from the ground than from its back. You should only get off your horse if you know that that will calm it down.

◊ Another solution to the problem is to turn around and ride another way.

◊ If there are several riders together and one of you has a problem with their horse, because it did not manage to get across with the rest of the group, you may carefully try to stop the traffic, so that the horse can get across. But be sure to stop the cars by giving a sign to the drivers. Do not try to stop the cars by simply riding out on the road.

Riding on slippery ground:

1. What is the risk?

Snow or ice on the road, mud on the riding path, or a wet lawn are all places that can be so slippery that the horse can slide if it is going in trot or canter. Most horses will not fall if only one leg slides out. But if it slides on two or more legs it may fall and, possibly, land on you.

To ride in snow can be a problem because the snow may cover holes in the ground, stones, branches, or other obstacles and make the horse stumble. Riding in melting snow on a horse with shoes can be difficult because the snow will collect under the hoof so that the horse may slide or stumble.

2. How can you avoid the risk?

◊ It is important to adjust the speed to the conditions which, most often, means to slow down to a walk. If it is very slippery it may be necessary to get off the horse and lead it. In that case, you need to keep a good distance from your horse, if it should fall anyway.

◊ If you are riding on a road with packed snow or ice, try to go out on the shoulder where the snow is looser.

◊ If you must ride on icy roads or wet lawns (for instance during a jumping competition), it may be necessary to screw studs into the shoes, that is, small metal taps that can 'bite' into the ground.

◊ If you ride in deep snow, you should only ride in trot or canter in places that you know well and where you know where the holes and the big stones are. In places that you are not familiar with, you should ride only in walk.

◊ To prevent melting snow from collecting under the hoof, it may help to smear hoof fat or, even better, hoof tar under the hoof. Another possibility is to get the farrier to fasten a horseshoe shaped rubber piece between hoof and shoe (a so-called snow-insole) that will prevent snow from piling up.

3. What should you do if your horse falls?

◊ If your horse falls, think of your own safety first. Try to get far enough away from the horse so that it does not step on you when it tries to get up. If it lands on the side and your leg is caught between horse and ground, try to pull out your leg as soon as the horse turns onto its chest.

◊ When you are free of the horse, try to calm it down by talking to it.

◊ If at all possible, keep hold of the reins and stand a little to the side of its head so that you still have it under control when it gets up. Do not stand right in front of it, so that it hits you when it gets up.

Riding up or down steep slopes:

1. What is the risk?

When you ride up or down steep slopes it can happen that the horse falls, that it does not have the strength to get all the way up, or that it is scared of going downhill. In all cases, there is a danger that it falls and lands on you.

2. What can you do to avoid an accident?

The most important thing to remember when riding on a slope is to ride perpendicularly to the slope. If the horse should lose its footing, it will not roll around but will still be able to keep upright.

When riding uphill you help the horse by leaning forward and standing in the stirrups so that it gets more freedom to use its back. When riding downhill it is best to lean backwards a little so that neither you nor the horse lose your balance forward. Both when you ride uphill and downhill, you should give your horse sufficiently loose reins so that it can use its head and neck freely. Be careful not to hang on the reins. Take hold of the mane or the front of the saddle to keep your balance.

Riding in darkness:

1. What is the risk?

◊ It is pretty obvious: the most dangerous aspect of riding in the dark is that others (for instance car drivers) cannot see horse and rider.

◊ But there are other aspects that make riding in darkness dangerous. First of all, neither horse nor rider can see where they are going so that they may bump into low hanging branches, step down into holes, or stumble over things on the path.

◊ Secondly, things look different in darkness which may scare the horse.

2. How can you avoid an accident?

◊ Both horse and rider should wear some reflective material. The rider should wear a reflective vest and the horse reflective bands on the legs. In addition, the rider should wear two lights, a white light on the chest that is visible from the front and a red light on the back visible from behind.

◊ Both horse and rider should know fairly well the terrain in which they ride. In addition, the speed should be so low (that is, walk), so that there is time to stop in case of a problem.

◊ The horse must be habituated to go in darkness. One way of doing so is to ride out at the end of the day so that it is dark during the last part of the ride home. Of course, this should only be done in a familiar area.

◊ If you wear a light on your chest, the horse must be habituated to the light beam. If the light is bouncing back and forth on the ground in front of it, it may get frightened.

3. What should you do if you are surprised by darkness?

◊ If you are out riding cross country without reflexive accessories or light and you do not manage to get home before darkness, you must be aware that car drivers and others may not be able to see you. Keep as far out to the side of the road as possible and avoid crossing roads unless cars are sufficiently far away.

◊   Remember that it may be necessary to call for help, for instance somebody who can escort you home with a bike or a car with light.

Stopping a horse that is bolting:

1. What is the risk?

> A horse that is bolting is, of course, a big danger, not only to itself and its rider but also to others. A horse that is bolting is obviously not under the rider's control but decides for itself where it is going and at what speed. Usually the reason why it is running is because it has become scared of something. Less often, the reason is that the horse is playful and just wants to get rid of some excess energy.
>
> A horse can accelerate incredibly fast. It is almost impossible to react fast enough to prevent it from running. Once it has gained speed, it is much more difficult to stop.

2. How can you prevent your horse from bolting?

> If you are fast enough to stop the horse before it gains speed, you have a much better chance to prevent it from bolting.
>
> Especially when you are hacking, you must keep an eye on the horse and on the surroundings. If you see something nearby that you know may frighten the horse, or if you notice that your horse becomes aware of something (for instance if it lifts its head, looks in a certain direction, or hesitates going forwards), you must be ready to react. Be ready to press your knees together and to stop your horse with the reins (see **Riding with loose reins,** page 129).

3. What can you do if your horse is bolting!

If your horse has managed to gain speed before you react, your strategy depends on the conditions. But one thing is certain in all cases: remain calm and do not shout. Shouting will only make your horse run faster.

If you are riding in open terrain and there is room for it, the best you can do is to ride your horse around in a circle. When a horse has to run in a circle, it has to slow down. If there is an area nearby with a soft ground (a newly ploughed field or something similar) that you can safely ride on, the heavy ground will soon make your horse tired.

If there is no room to ride your horse around in a circle, you may try to steer it towards something big and solid that can stop your horse. It could be a building or a tall thick hedge. It is, however, important that it is an obstacle that is sufficiently solid so that the horse does not try to force its way through. You also have to be aware of the conditions of the ground so that your horse does not slide, for instance on asphalt.

If your horse does not react to a 'normal' pull on the reins, it may help to pull the reins alternately, that is to change between pulling the right and the left rein (also referred to as 'sawing' – to be used only in an emergency). But be careful not to pull so much that the horse turns its head too much to the side, or so that it raises its head and does not see where it is going.

Many horses have a tendency to go faster on the way home than on the way out. And horses have a really good sense of direction. Often you can feel the difference as soon as the direction is towards home, even in places where the horse has never been before.

If your horse is very keen on getting home and if you are afraid that it may take control, you should avoid the faster gaits on the way back and only ride in canter on the way out.

If the horse continuously increases its speed and, for instance, constantly starts trotting, bring it down into a walk by exerting tension on the reins and bracing the muscles of your abdomen. Remember the most important thing, to release the tension as soon as the horse complies. If it then starts to trot again, repeat stopping it and continue to do so as long as it is necessary.

It is important to release the pressure every time you have slowed down the horse. Pulling constantly on the reins will never teach the horse to walk calmly (see **Stopping a horse and making it go forward, page 70**)

Helping a rider who has fallen off a horse:

1.   What is the risk?

There is always a risk involved when a rider falls off a horse when you are out riding. The rider can be seriously hurt and in need of medical attention. The horse can get loose and be on its way towards a busy road. The other horses may be agitated. The other riders may be nervous.

2. What should you do?

The first thing you must do is to help the rider. If it looks as if she is seriously hurt, you must call for emergency help (see **Mobile phone** (page 28) and **First aid** (page 82)). The next thing is to try to catch the loose horse. But do not ride or run after it. That may just make it run even further away. If it is in familiar terrain it may run back to the stable. If it is in unknown terrain it will probably stop after a short while and, possibly, come back to the other horses. If it is on its way towards a dangerous place, such as a busy road, try to get its attention and ride away from the road in an attempt to make it follow you.

If the other horses (and riders) are nervous, remember to remain calm. Yelling will only create more panic, so it is important to remain as calm as possible.

Riding away from other horses:

1. What is the risk?

Even though it is safest never to ride out alone, it can sometimes be necessary to have to ride away from other horses, for instance if you have to go and get help for an injured rider. But to leave other horses is something your horse must learn. As described under Horse behaviour horses are herd animals that prefer to join up with completely strange horses rather than being alone.

Horses that do not mind going out alone may still react to being left by other horses during the ride. To be able to go away from the stable alone is not the same as being left on the trail.

In addition, some horses get agitated when they meet other, unfamiliar horses during the ride, probably because they would prefer to join them (see **Meeting other riders,** page 158).

2. How can you reduce the risk?

You have to teach your horse to go away from other horses. The safest way is to start the training in the riding arena and only to separate the horses for a short time in the beginning. If your horse reacts strongly, it may be safer to lead it than to ride it. .

As you repeat the training you can gradually make the separation last longer, for instance by riding further and further away from each other, before joining up again. Later, you also have to train outdoors, both to separate near the stable and out on the trail.

Meeting other riders:

1. What is the risk?

◊ Horses are herd animals. They prefer to join completely unfamiliar horses rather than being alone. To meet other horses on the ride can make an untrained horse very agitated.

◊ Horses that run can scare a horse. To pass other riders in full gallop may make the other horses charge.

◊ Horses that sniff each other will often react by squealing and by striking with a front leg (see **When horses meet each other,** page 45).

2. How can you avoid an accident?

◊ You should habituate your horse to meet other horses during the ride, both familiar and unfamiliar horses. Also horses that usually only go out together with other horses should learn to be separated. It could happen that it became necessary to ride it home alone. (See also **Riding away from other horses,** page 157)

◊ You must always pass other riders only in walk. Any other gait is impolite. It is important that we show each other consideration.

◊ If you meet riders who are going in the same direction as you are, and you want to get by because you go faster, you must always first ask permission to do so.

3. What should you do if other riders do not show consideration?

If you meet or are passed by other riders that do not know the rules for good behaviour and your horse gets nervous, you can ride it as you do when it is charging, that is ride it around in a circle. If you want to be absolutely certain that the situation should not constitute a risk, you can actually habituate your horse to being passed by other horses cantering. Preferably, you should start the training in the riding arena before you go out and train it cross country.

Meeting other people in the countryside:

1. What is the risk?

◊ When you ride cross country you must be aware of other people and show them consideration. Not only may they frighten your horse; they may also be frightened *by* your horse.

◊ Horses are not always able to recognize people wearing a backpack or a big bag or people pushing a stroller in front of them or hiding behind an umbrella, all something that can frighten a horse.

◊ A mountain bike that comes speeding by may easily cause the horse to jump to the side.

◊ Kindergarten kids and school children on a tour in the woods are often thrilled (and loud) when meeting a horse. Although your horse is usually not afraid of children, the number of them and the noise level may scare it anyway.

2. How do you avoid an accident?

◊ When you meet people nearby, you should pull up and let them walk by. In that way your horse has a better chance at looking at them and is less likely to be frightened. If necessary, you might make the people aware that you are coming.

◊ If you ride in a dense wood you should be aware that somebody else might use the path you are riding on, possibly also pedestrians even though you are on a riding path. If the path passes around dense vegetation, you should slow down and be prepared to stop. You should only ride at a fast gallop where vision allows it.

◊ If you meet people with baby buggies or something similar and you notice that your horse is getting tense, you should react in the same way as when approaching something scary (see **Riding past scary things**, page 147). If possible, ride by with as much distance as possible. If it is not possible, perhaps you could ask the people to stand still. Remember, in this situation you should not only think of your own safety, but also of the safety of other people.

◊ Unfortunately, not all mountain bike riders show consideration of others on their way cross country. Therefore, you need to be alert in areas where they ride. If you see a mountain bike approaching, turn your horse so that it has a chance to see the bike.

◊ If a group of happy children are running towards you to say hi to the horse, you need to warn them that your horse might kick. Even if it is not really your responsibility, you will still get the blame if a child should get hurt.

Riding where insects attack:

1. What is the risk?

    Some horses are very sensitive to attacks from insects. A bee swarm can actually make a group of horses run wildly. If several riders and horses are going together, it can be hard to keep control over the group. Horseflies or mosquitoes can also agitate the horses.

2. How can you reduce the risk?

    The most effective way to keep insects at a distance is to trot or canter at a moderate speed, so that they cannot settle down on the horses. Another way is to break off a small branch with leaves on and to use it as a flyswatter. Just be careful not to scare the horse with it. Use it gently the first couple of times.

Riding by pastures with cattle, pigs, and other animals:

1. What is the risk?

    When you are riding past a herd of cattle in a pasture, chances are that they come running up to you because they are curious. It is not only other horses running that can make a horse nervous. Also other animals running can agitate a horse (for instance cattle, deer etc.). Free range pigs are usually less curious, but some horses still get scared of them.

2. How can you reduce the risk?

    It is obvious that the slower you go (that is walk) and the greater the distance to the pasture, the calmer your horse will be. Apart from that you should approach the animals the same way you approach other scary things (see **Riding past scary things,** page 147). Be patient. Give the horse a chance to look at the animals. When you do that, the animals may also calm down.

    If you have to pass the pasture often you should consider doing a little more habituation, not only of your horse but also of the animals in the pasture. Spend 5–10 minutes on riding back and forth past the pasture, until it gets to be uninteresting for the animals and repeat it a couple of days later, possibly several times.

Riding through water:

1. What is the risk?

   If you are cantering through the country and your horse suddenly jumps a metre sideways to avoid stepping in a puddle, you can easily lose your balance and fall off. Therefore, it is a good idea to habituate your horse to go through water. The reason why horses avoid water is not that they are scared of water but rather that they cannot see the bottom where they have to step, and that makes them insecure.

2. How can you reduce the risk?

   You should habituate your horse to going through water the same way you habituate it to other things (see for instance **Training your horse to go over things,** page 77). Start with a small puddle and ride in walk or trot. Also let the horse stop up for a moment in the middle of the puddle, so that it learns not to rush through. Use the opportunity to practise on the puddles you meet on your ride, also the bigger and deeper ones, and when you are cantering.

Habituating your horse to sounds:

1. What is the risk?

◊ Many horses become scared when something moves and makes a sound in a bush or in the undergrowth in the forest, for instance birds or small mammals fleeing. Many horses will react by jumping to the side or by turning around and running away.

◊ Some horses may be scared by sounds coming from the rider, possibly because they come from an unusual direction. It may be the sound of a zipper being opened or closed, the sound of a raincoat blowing in the wind, the sound of a plastic bag of sweets being opened, or of a bottle of soft drink being opened.

2. How can you prevent the problem?

◊ As described under **Habituation** you may not be able to teach your horse not to get scared. But to some extent you can teach it not to show flight behaviour when it gets scared.

◊ If you expose your horse to various sounds during your ride once in a while, it will get used to the sounds after a number of repetitions and stop reacting to them.

◊ You can make different sounds by having small stones or short pieces of branches in your pocket that you throw into a bush or into the undergrowth.

◊ If you know that your horse reacts strongly to sounds, you may want to lead your horse instead of riding it. Make sure that the horse does not jump into you if it should react. (See also **Habituating your horse to dogs** (page 80) in the section **Applied training** (page 74).)

◊ If you do not want your horse to react to sounds coming from somewhere above his back, you should habituate it to different sounds. The safest way is to start the habituation from the ground, preferably while a helper is holding the horse. Stand in front of the horse, slightly to the side and make a sound, for instance from plastic being squeezed, and gradually move it up over the withers of the horse. If it tries to escape, do not stop making the sound. Instead, continue to make the sound, preferably a short distance from the horse. Not until it is standing still can you stop the sound. If you stop the sound while the horse is trying to escape, you will teach it that it just has to run away to stop the sound, which is the exact opposite of what you want to teach it.

3. How can you avoid an accident if your horse gets scared?

◊ The most important thing is to be prepared, if your horse should jump to the side or turn around and run. The best preparation is to press your knees against the saddle and to sit deep in the saddle.

◊ In addition, you should either ride with loose reins that you hold with one hand (see **Riding with loose reins,** page 129), or you should hold one rein in each hand and have light contact with the horse's mouth so that you are able to stop the horse before it runs.

◊ To eat sweets, to drink a soft drink, to smoke a cigarette, or other similar activities on the back of a horse is a bad idea. Apart from the fact that the sound of paper or plastic may frighten the horse, a sudden movement may make you inhale your sweets, drop your cigarette, spray fluid in the face of the horse, or similar accidents. And if you are sitting fumbling with a bag or a bottle or a lighter, you do not have your hands free to stop your horse if it should start running.

Chapter 12

Riding problem horses

Warning:

◊   Horses that show serious behaviour problems are not suited for beginners nor even for more experienced riders. It can be necessary to get professional help to solve a problem.

◊   Not all behaviour problems can be solved. In some cases it may be necessary to have a horse euthanized.

◊   To sell a horse with a serious behaviour problem without mentioning the problem to the new owner is highly irresponsible because it may jeopardize the lives of other people.

◊   The reason for a behaviour problem may be physical, such as a pain in the back or in other areas. Therefore, a horse with a behaviour problem needs to be checked by a veterinarian.

Why horses show problem behaviour:

> ## No horse is born with a behaviour problem

In most cases (maybe in all?) the reason for a behaviour problem is due to the fact that the horse has been treated wrongly and that it has been subjected to a conflict situation. The only way the horse can solve a conflict is to react in a certain way that, usually, is a problem for us.

What is conflict behaviour?
    If an animal is motivated to show two behavioural reactions that are mutually exclusive, it may choose a third kind of behavioural reaction.

Example 1

A cat meets another cat. The cat is motivated to attack and chase the other cat away plus it is motivated to flee so that it will not get attacked. Instead, it sits down and grooms itself. The cat cannot decide what to do (to attack or to run away) and, therefore, chooses an unrelated type of behaviour. (We people do the same when we cannot answer a question. We scratch our head).

Example 2

A horse normally learns to go forward on the pressure from the rider's legs and to stop on the pressure of the bit. But if the rider attempts to collect the horse by simultaneously pressing with the legs and stopping it with the reins, the horse is exposed to two signals in opposite directions. The horse is exposed to a conflict situation. To solve the problem, the horse tries a different kind of behaviour by rearing, by bolting, or something similar. (See also **Collecting a horse,** page 131).

Example 3

A young horse is frightened by something, for instance a jacket hanging on the railing of the riding arena. It tries to yield to the side to avoid the scary thing, but the rider punishes the horse for not going straight. The horse's belief that the thing was dangerous is confirmed because it is hit by a whip near the place. Next time it goes by the place it reacts even more strongly and is, yet again, punished. When the episode has been repeated enough times the horse gives up, rears or bucks or reacts in an otherwise uncontrolled manner. The rider concludes that the horse is crazy and dangerous to ride.

A typical situation that can cause a conflict in a horse is if it receives a signal from the rider that it does not understand. If in addition the horse is punished for not obeying, it gets even more confused. The only way it can solve its problem is by trying to avoid it all by rearing or running away.

> **To punish a horse that does not understand the signal that the rider is giving, does not improve the horse's understanding. On the contrary.**

Another matter is if the horse bucks or bolts because of excess energy, for instance because it has been standing in its stable for some time. It can be difficult to decide whether it reacts because it is scared or playful. The best way to deal with the situation is to stop its behaviour (for instance by stopping it or by changing direction) and then make it go forward again. Your reaction should be something in between calming it down and stopping its play.

Riding a horse that rears:

1. What is the risk?

An experienced horse that rears usually knows how much it can get up on its hind legs without losing its balance, even when it has a rider on its back.

A less experienced horse is in greater danger of losing its balance because of the rider and of falling over backwards. Obviously, it can be extremely dangerous if it falls over backwards and lands on the rider.

2. What should you do to prevent the horse from rearing?

    A horse is more likely to rear if it is driven forward towards something that it is afraid of approaching.

    If the horse hesitates to go forward and you know that it has a tendency to rear, or if it shows signs of wanting to rear (for instance by getting up a little bit), try to turn it into another direction. As soon as it goes forward you can gradually approach the place again.

3. What should you do if the horse rears?

    a.   Give the horse longer reins. Be sure that you do not pull on the reins.

    b.   Lean forward and try to push the horse down with your weight

    c.   If you feel that the horse may fall over backwards (or if you are afraid that it could happen), take hold of the front of the saddle, take your feet out of the stirrups, swing your right leg over the horse's back, and jump down

◊   **Release the reins**

◊   **Hold on to the mane or saddle**

◊   **Press tight with your knees**

◊   **Lean forward**

If your horse only rears a little or if you feel reasonably safe in the saddle, you may try to turn the horse to the side (and usually turning it to the left is most effective). For one thing, the pull on the left rein will give your horse something new to think about. For another, the movement to the side will inhibit

Above all else, you must not pull on the reins because it can make the horse fall over backwards

the movement upwards somewhat, so that it is less likely to rear. As soon as the horse 'lands again', drive it forward. To keep the horse moving will reduce the risk that it will rear again.

If your horse has learned to 'solve problems' by rearing, you have to realize that you have a dangerous horse. Unless you are a very experienced rider, you need professional help to correct the behaviour problem. Selling the horse and not telling the new owner about its problem is outright irresponsible. In fact, euthanasia may be the only (sad) solution to the problem.

Riding a horse that bucks:

1. What is the risk?

   A horse bucks by lowering its head almost to the ground, arching its back, lifting its hind end, and by jumping up in the air on stiff legs. The sudden movement upwards throws the rider up in the air. The horse 'lands' on the ground before the rider. If it bucks a second time right after the first time, it means that the rider lands on the horse as it is 'going up'. Needless to say, it is rather difficult to stay on the horse during such a series of buck springs. The risk of falling off is great.

2. What can you do to prevent the horse from bucking?

    A prerequisite for bucking is that the horse lowers its head. If you can manage to keep its head high, it will not be able to buck. At the same time you must try to drive it forwards with your legs to keep it in the gait in which it was going. As soon as it stops trying to buck you should stop it and walk a few metres, thereafter in trot and possibly canter.

3. What should you do if the horse bucks?

a. Press your legs as much as possible around the horse and try to sit deep in the saddle

b. Lean back and follow the movements of the horse as well as possible. Be careful not to fall forwards

c. Pull its head up, possibly with a 'sawing' motion (only to be used in emergencies)

d. Drive the horse energetically forwards and then stop it to a walk

Riding a horse that kicks:

1. What is the risk?

    A horse that kicks out after other horses, after people or something else, obviously always constitutes a risk. It can hit and hurt other horses or their rider.

    Some horses react by kicking if they are punished with a whip or spurs, or if the rider uses a whip or spurs to drive them forward.

    A horse can kick with one or both hind legs because it is aggressive and wants to chase away an enemy (another horse, a person, a dog, or something similar) in self-defence.

    But a horse can also kick with a front leg, for instance when two horses meet and stand sniffing each other. In that situation, you should not stand right in front of the horse.

    In general, you should never stand right in front of a horse, especially not if you or somebody else (for instance a veterinarian) does something to the horse that it does not like. (See **Working around a horse,** page 108)

2. How can you prevent your horse from kicking?

    First of all, it is important to keep a distance from other horses and people. Secondly, you must warn people in your surroundings that your horse has the bad habit of kicking so that they also keep at a distance. (In the UK many people tie a red ribbon round the top of their horse's tail to warn people about a kicker.)

    If it is necessary to punish your horse with a whip or with spurs, (see **Whip,** page 57, **Punishment,** page 56, and **Spurs,** 134), you must only do so if nobody is too close to you.

3. What should you do if your horse kicks?

    It can be very difficult to eradicate the bad habit of kicking, especially if the horse kicks out of fear. If your horse is aggressive towards one specific horse, it may help to place them, first, in stables or pastures next to each other, later to let them out in the pasture together. In that way they may solve their conflict without your interference.

    If it is only in the riding arena that your horse is aggressive towards other horses, you may try to change its behaviour by letting another horse and rider pass you, in the beginning at some distance, thereafter with less and less distance. If your horse shows no reaction, praise it with a stroke on the withers. If it reacts aggressively (by turning back its ears or kicking out), respond with a sharp 'no' and drive it forwards. In that way, there is a chance that your horse learns to accept that other horses pass it.

Riding stallions:

Stallions do not necessarily have behaviour problems. They just show their natural behaviour a little more clearly than mares and geldings. What this means is that riding a stallion is somewhat more demanding than riding mares and geldings. What it also means is that riding a stallion is absolutely not for beginners.

By nature, a stallion is 'programmed' to collect a harem of mares that he can keep together and mount when they are in heat. To be able to do so, he needs to keep other stallions away. This behaviour is pretty much innate. Only a little learning is involved.

Under natural conditions, a stallion will circle around the mares to get them into a group if another stallion approaches. Only then will he go out towards the other stallion, either to scare him away or to fight with him.

If other dangers threaten, for instance attacks from carnivores, he may also attack. If he feels a threat from people, and for instance thinks they will steal his mares, he may also attack people. Obviously, this can cause an extremely dangerous situation.

> **Remember:**
> **Stallions are not for beginners. Stallions can attack people**
> **if they feel threatened.**

To work with and to ride a stallion therefore requires special demands of the rider.

First of all, you must be aware that a stallion is more 'extrovert' and most often will try to approach other horses, either to collect mares for his harem or to fight with them.

Secondly, a stallion is more likely to show his innate behaviour so that the learned behaviour is somewhat suppressed. For that reason it is even more important to be consistent when training and working with a stallion and always insist that he shows the correct behavioural reactions to the different signals.

On the other hand, if you are consistent in your training of a stallion and if you avoid certain situations (such as mares in heat), a stallion is no more difficult to work with or to ride than any other horse.

Stallions are often more aware of their surroundings which can make it easier to work with them. If there is no distractions in the surroundings (such as mares), they learn just as fast as other horses. They are often less likely to get scared.

The habits that a stallion has formed will stay with him even if he is castrated. Castration of a stallion will remove part of his motivation to collect mares and chase away other stallions, but part of the behaviour can remain a long time after the castration.

When stallions fight they mostly try to bite each other on the neck and chest. In addition, they may 'box' each other, that is, kick each other with the front legs. When a stallion sniffs another horse, the meeting will often result in a strike with a front leg while rearing. In that situation you must never stand right in front of the stallion.

◊   Always keep a large distance from other horses

◊   Be careful when a stallion sniffs another horse. Usually the meeting ends with a squeal and a strike with a front leg

◊   Be extra careful in maintaining good habits and correcting bad habits from the very beginning if a stallion starts to show them

◊   If the stallion is kept together with mares, be aware that he may defend them and become aggressive towards you

Riding mares in season

Mares in heat may change behaviour. They are more likely to lift their tail and they are more likely to urinate. Some mares may change character in that they become more aggressive towards other horses and, possibly, towards people. Their aggression they may show by biting or by kicking. Therefore, it is important to keep an extra distance from other horses and to warn people not to get too close. If you are riding together with stallions, obviously, it is especially important to let their riders know about the condition of your mare, whether it is aggressive or not.

Chapter 13

Trailer and lorry transportation of horses

TRANSPORTATION of a horse in a trailer or horse lorry is an activity in which the risk of having an accident is high. Most horses do not like to go into a small space. Transportation often means participation in competitions or that a strict time schedule must be followed. Both facts mean that you are somewhat nervous and apprehensive and maybe not quite as patient as usual. The diversion from the daily schedule makes your horse even more hesitant to enter the trailer. Your horse's hesitation and your lack of patience may easily result in a bit of a fight.

An important requirement for avoiding an accident during trailer transportation is that trailer loading of your horse becomes a routine. The training to establish this routine must be done at a time when you do not have to go anywhere, and when you have lots of time and are not restricted by a tight schedule.

> **Training of your horse in trailer loading should not be done on the day you are going to a competition or on summer vacation with your horse. The training should be done on days before the transportation, when you are not going anywhere.**

Equipment:

You need to wear solid footwear. The risk that the horse takes a step to the side and steps on you is even greater than usual.

You should wear gloves so that you have a good grip on the lead rope. The risk that the horse pulls back is greater during trailer loading than usual.

The horse should be led in a halter with a lead rope. To prevent it from getting hurt from stepping down over the side of the ramp, it is a good idea to put bandages on its legs.

The following description refers to a two-horse trailer.

Hitching a trailer to the car:

1. What is the risk?

When the hitch of the trailer is placed on the hook of the car, it is possible that it ends up lying on top of the hook, instead of clamping down around the hook.

If you are in a hurry, you may forget to connect the cable that brakes the trailer, to raise the support wheel of the trailer, or to check the lights, stop lights, and turn signals of the trailer.

2. How can you avoid the risk?

When you place the trailer hitch on the trailer hook of the car correctly, an indicator shows that the hitch clamps around the hook.

To be completely sure that the connection is correct, you can try to lift the front end of the trailer. If the car 'follows', the trailer hitch is placed correctly.

When the trailer is hitched on you must

1. connect the brake cable of the trailer to the hook of the car
2. connect the electric cable of the trailer to the socket of the car
3. lift the support wheel of the trailer
4. check lights, turn signals, and stop lights on the trailer

Before you drive off you should check around the trailer that all doors and ramps are closed and locked, and that possible blocks under the wheels of the trailer are removed. And when you start driving, it is a good idea to look in the back mirror and check that the trailer is actually following!

Leading a horse into the trailer:

1. What is the risk?

A horse that does not go straight into the trailer can easily get too close to the edge of the ramp. If it slides down the edge it can hurt its leg.

A horse that has entered the trailer can easily regret going in, and back out again.

A horse that is tied in front, before the bar behind it is fastened, can pull back and break the rope or the halter with the result that it rears up and falls over.

2. How can you reduce the risk?

An excited horse that does not go straight into the trailer should have bandages on its legs, before it is loaded. It can be a good idea to park the trailer parallel with and close to a wall, so that the horse can only deviate to one side.

The only way effectively to keep the horse in the trailer is to fasten the bar behind the horse. It is important to fasten it *before* the horse is tied in front.

Before you start loading the horse, the trailer should be attached to the car. A loose trailer can easily tip or roll off if it is not attached to a car.

Before loading the horse, you should open the front door in the trailer. For one thing, it will make the space lighter so that the horse is more likely to go in. For another, and more importantly, you will have an emergency exit if the horse creates problems inside the trailer.

Summary – to lead an experienced horse into the trailer:

1. Open ramp and front door
2. Lead the horse with a lead rope up the ramp
3. Let the horse go into the trailer while you remain standing next to the ramp
4. As the horse goes by, place the rope over the horse's neck so that it does not step on the rope
5. When the horse is inside, place the bar behind the horse
6. Lock the bar with a split pin
7. Go in through the front door and tie up the horse
8. Go back and shut the ramp

Summary – to lead a less experienced horse into the trailer:

1. Open the ramp and front door
2. Lead the horse with a lead rope up the ramp
3. Go in front of the horse into the trailer
4. When the horse is inside, get a helper to place the bar behind the horse
5. Tie up the horse in front
6. Close the ramp

When the bar behind the horse is placed in its holder, it must be secured with a split pin. If you do not do so, the horse can force the bar up and out of the holder. When the bar swings down it can scare the horse. In addition, the horse may pull out as soon as the ramp is opened.

'Emergency' loading of a horse into the trailer:

It is not unusual to see 'difficult' horses (that is, horses that have not received proper training) being loaded by tying two ropes or lunge lines to either side of the trailer and having two people bring the ropes around behind the horse, so that the ropes cross each other. The procedure should absolutely only be used in an emergency situation.

If you try to use it, make sure that the ropes are placed on the thighs of the horse, so that it does not get the ropes tangled around its feet. The ropes should stop the horse from yielding out to the side. In addition, it is possible to pull the horse forward with both ropes.

Some horses will kick with their hind legs when they feel the ropes on their thighs. The two helpers should keep a good distance from the horse.

> Note: This method should only be used in an emergency situation. A much better procedure is to train trailer loading as described later.

> **An important prerequisite is that trailer loading is done in as calm a way as possible, without fighting and excitement. To punish the horse in this situation does not increase the probability that the horse will enter the trailer.**
> **On the contrary.**

Tying up a horse in the trailer:

1. What is the risk?

◊   If a horse is tied up before the bar is fastened behind it, the horse may try to pull back and either break the rope or the halter and fall over backwards.

◊   If the bar is not locked in place with a split pin, a horse or especially a pony can push it up and away by going backwards. If the horse is not yet tied up, it will be able to get out of the trailer. If it is tied up in front, it may break the rope or the halter, rear, and fall over backwards.

◊   The bar behind the horse should sit at a level so that it reaches the horse in the middle of the thighs. If it sits higher, for instance near the tail, the horse can press the bar out of its holder. If smaller ponies are transported, it may be necessary to have the bar lowered.

◊   If a nervous horse is tied too loosely, it may try to jump up over the front bar.

◊   If two horses are transported in the trailer, they may bite each other if they are tied too loosely.

   2.   How can you reduce the risk?

◊   The horse must not be tied up until the bar behind it has been fastened and locked in position with a split pin, so that the horse cannot push up the bar.

◊   The horse should be tied so tightly that it cannot get its head above the level it normally carries its head. The rope should be brought down under the front bar, before it is tied to the side of the trailer. In that way the horse cannot raise its head too high. Therefore, it is less likely to try to jump over the front bar.

◊   If two horses are transported together, they must be tied up so tightly that they can just barely sniff each other but not otherwise reach each other.

   3.   What should you do if an accident happens?

◊   If the horse starts to pull backwards while it is tied up and while there is no bar behind it, leave the trailer through its side door. Do not leave by going along the horse. If you can manage to get behind the trailer, try to move the horse forward, for instance by waving a jacket or something behind it, in the same way as described under **Tying up a horse** (page 105). But be careful not to get too close to the horse if the rope should break and the horse fall over backwards. If you succeed in stopping the horse, make sure that you put up the bar behind it immediately, before going up in front.

Driving with a trailer:

   1.   What is the risk?

◊   A nervous horse standing in a trailer that is not moving is more likely to try to get out.

◊   Sudden stops, sharp turns, and fast driving over bumps or through roundabouts all makes it difficult for the horse to keep its balance, which makes it unsteady.

2.   How can you reduce the risk?

◊   The more carefully you drive with the trailer, the less uncomfortable it is for the horse and the greater the chance that the horse will go up into the trailer next time.

◊   Every change in direction or speed of the trailer should be done as softly as possible.

◊   Drive carefully around corners.

◊   Keep a distance from cars ahead to avoid sudden stops.

◊   Drive slowly over bumps, so that the horse does not lose its balance.

As long as the trailer is moving, the horse is busy keeping its balance. Many horses get nervous when the trailer stands still. Therefore, avoid longer breaks while underway, unless you know that your horse can stand still in the trailer.

As soon as you have got your horse up into the trailer, placed the bar behind it, tied it up, and closed the ramp and side door, you should start driving. This means that all other equipment and other stuff that you need for the trip should be loaded onto the car before you load the horse into the trailer. In that way you can avoid the horse standing waiting unnecessarily.

Leading a horse out of the trailer:

1.   What is the risk?

◊   If the horse has got loose during the drive (for instance because the hook on the rope has a panic release) or if it has removed the bar behind it, it may start going backwards while you open the ramp. You can get seriously hurt if you get the ramp down over you.

◊   If your horse gets nervous when the trailer is standing still, it may try to get out by jumping over the front bar. If you have two horses in the trailer, they may start to fight with each other.

◊   If your horse is very keen on getting out of the trailer, it may try to turn around while it is on its way down the ramp with the result that it steps over the edge of the ramp and hurts its leg.

◊   If there are two horses in the trailer, number two may get very impatient when number one is unloaded.

    2.   What should you do to avoid an accident?

When the drive is over (or if you take a break during the drive) you should open the side door and check if everything is ok. You especially need to see if the bar behind the horse is in place. If you unload the horse right away, untie it and put the rope over its neck. Not until then should you or a helper open the ramp.

If your horse is very agitated you should stay with it while a helper opens ramp and bar.

When you lead the horse out, make sure that it is going straight down the ramp. If it turns its hind end to the side, turn its head to the same side so that it cannot yield out too far.

If the horse that is taken out as number two is very nervous, a person must stay with it to calm it down. Next time you unload the horses, you should take that one out first.

Unloading an experienced horse from the trailer:

    1.   Untie the horse and place the rope over its neck
    2.   Remove the bar behind it and give it a sign to go out
    3.   Stand on the ramp, so that you can guide the horse straight out
    4.   As it is going by, you take the rope from its neck

Unloading a less experienced horse from the trailer:

    1.   Untie the horse and hold it with the rope
    2.   Get a helper to remove the bar behind it
    3.   Give the horse a signal to go backwards as you are walking out with the horse
    4.   Have your helper stand next to the ramp so he can help guiding the horse straight out

Training the horse in trailer loading:

Remember

◊   The horse must go up the ramp in a straight line

◊   The horse must go down the ramp in a straight line

◊   The horse must learn to go halfway up the ramp, to stand still on the ramp, and then to continue up the ramp

◊   The horse must learn to go halfway down the ramp, to stand still on the ramp, and then to go forward on the ramp again

It is important that a horse learns from the beginning to go in and out of the trailer in a calm way. To achieve that, it is necessary to teach it to stop both on the way in and on the way out, to wait a few seconds, and then to continue going in or out. In that way, the horse learns to obey the signals to stop and to go forward, also on the ramp of the trailer.

1. Teach your horse to go forward (see **Teaching the horse to go forward,** page 68)
2. If necessary, first teach the horse to go over ramps (see **Training your horse to go over things,** page 77)
3. Lead your horse up to the ramp. If necessary, use the whip to tap it forward. (see **Whip,** page 57)
4. Give the horse time to check out the ramp. Be patient.
5. Stop the horse halfway up the ramp. Make it stand still and maybe go back a couple of steps. In that way the process is not as hectic and it is easier to habituate the horse to go up and down the ramp.
6. When the horse is all the way inside the trailer, wait a moment without placing the bar behind it and make it back out again. In that way it learns to stand still in the trailer, also when it is not tied up.
7. Repeat the trip several times, both up and down the ramp, until the horse is completely familiar with the procedure.

Conclusion

THERE are no 'magic bullets' when it comes to avoiding accidents. This is true for all aspects of life and it is true when working with horses. Consequently, in order to stay healthy and happy as a horse person it is necessary to pay attention to numerous little things. It is not enough to put a riding helmet on your head. Some of 'the little things' you need to pay attention to are described in the second part of the book **Applied Information**. For more than 70 situations that may occur when you work with your horse and when you ride, it is described why the situation may be risky, what you should do (or not do) to prevent an accident, and in some cases what you can do if an accident should happen. Of course, knowing about a risk and knowing what to do to prevent an accident is by far the best strategy for safety.

Apart from knowing about these many risk factors, an important aspect of riding safety is to learn about horse behaviour in general and the behaviour of *your* horse specifically. Obviously, if you want to stand close to or sit on such a strong animal, the more you know about how it reacts in many different situations, the better you will be able to prepare yourself for its reactions. You need to know how horses in general experience their surroundings through their senses and how they process the information they get. This knowledge you can get by reading the chapter on horse behaviour. Some of this information is the same for all horses but when it comes to the way they respond there is a lot of variation between horses. Therefore, you must also learn how *your* horse reacts and you must find out which specific things *your* horse is afraid of. A good and safe way to find out about this is by doing the habituation exercises described in the chapter on training.

Another important aspect of riding safety is to establish good habits. Both people and horses function better when the things we do become routine. If you always stop your horse before going through a door or a gate, the idea of rushing through will never occur to your horse. But the routine does not mean that you always do everything the same way. The horse must learn to stand still when you give it the signal to stop. It must learn to do so wherever you stop it, in the riding arena, when you groom and saddle it, when you take a break on the trail ride, etc. Its response to your signals must be the same no matter where you give them. That also means that part of the habit formation is not just teaching your horse good habits. It is just as much you who have to develop good habits. If you want your horse to obey you, you need to tell the horse what you want from it. If you want it to stand still, you must give it the signal to do so. You cannot just assume that it will do so on its own.

Developing habits and doing things according to a routine does not mean that you should not pay attention to what you are doing. Being a prey animal by nature a horse is always extremely aware of its surroundings, constantly smelling, hearing and seeing what goes on. You must do the same thing. It is all right to sit relaxed on the horse and chat with your fellow rider during the ride, but you still have to pay attention to your horse as well as to things happening around you. Paying attention means that you can react a fraction of a second earlier than if you do not pay attention. Your fast reaction may mean that you are able to stay in the saddle instead of falling off or that you are able to get out of the way instead of getting kicked.

Probably the most important aspect when working with horses is to do so in a calm and goal-directed way. Some people believe that it is necessary to 'dominate' the horse or to be the 'leader' or the 'alpha animal' in order to get the horse to 'respect' the rider or trainer. This is complete nonsense. When a horse is confronted with an aggressive individual – a horse or a person – its reaction is to avoid the opponent, to get away from the conflict situation. And that is exactly the response that we do not want because then the horse will not be motivated to learn anything. If instead you carry out the training in a calm, non-aggressive, and 'non-dominating' manner your horse will be much more motivated to work for you. But besides being calm you need to behave in a goal-directed way. You need to have a clear idea of what you are going to do next. Whether you groom or saddle the horse, lead it or sit on its back you must show the horse with your body language what you are going to do in the next few seconds. The information that you send to the horse in this way means that it will also remain calm and it will mean that it is much more likely to behave the way you expect it to behave.

Safety (or risk) is a matter of probability. If you do not think about it at all, the probability that you will experience an accident is relatively high. But of course, it does not necessarily mean that you will have an accident. Similarly, if you do what you can to avoid an accident, the probability that you will have one is relatively low. But of course, it does not necessarily mean that you will be home free. Unfortunately there is no guarantee that something might happen. It only means that the probability is less.

Suggested reading

Of the thousands of books on horses and horseback riding I particularly recommend the following:

Andrew McLean (2003) *The Truth About Horses* Quarto Publishing plc.
Daniel Mills & Sue McDonnell (2005) *The Domestic Horse* Cambridge University Press.
Lesley Skipper (2008) *Exercise School for Horse and Rider* New Holland Publishing Ltd.
George H. Waring (2003) *Horse Behavior* William Andrew Publishing.

Index

Entries in **bold** denote an illustration

Lightning Source UK Ltd.
Milton Keynes UK
UKHW051605060520
362677UK00003B/11